THE SECRET LIVES
Of
TONY F IN' Z
Or
EL GUERRO QUE VENGA LOS NINO'S
(The Warrior That Avenges the Children)

Front cover illustration by Sensei Craig Maher, commercial artist

Front cover design by Saiko Sensei Tony Zeno

Book design by Saiko Sensei Tony Zeno

Edited by Saiko Sensei Tony Zeno, Head of KYOKUNINJAKAN KARATE

First printing by Draft2Digital USA, 2023

Saiko Sensei Tony Zeno is the highest ranking Black Belt (Head Sensei) in the KYOKUNINJAKAN KARATE system, which includes Karate, Jujitsu, Aikido & Bando.

<u>(SO DON"T PISS HIM OFF!!!)</u>

While every precaution has been taken in the preparation of this book, the publisher assumes no responsibility for errors or omissions, or for damages resulting from the use of the information contained herein.

THE SECRET LIVES OF TONY F IN'Z

First edition, September 26, 2023

Copyright 2023 Tony F N'Z

ISBN: 979-8223777038

Written by Tony F N'Z

While every precaution has been taken in the preparation of this book, the publisher assumes no responsibility for errors or omissions, or for damages resulting from the use of the information contained herein.

THE SECRET LIVES OF TONY F IN'Z

First edition. September 26, 2023.

Copyright © 2023 Tony F N' Z.

ISBN: 979-8223777038

Written by Tony F N' Z.

This book is a small summery (more to come) of the "true" events and adventures in the life of the author. It reflects over 75 years of actual happy, crazy to tragic events and adventures in my life. Many are humorous, sexy and/or tragic, but all are true. Most I have kept secret for various and some obvious reasons from family, friends and students. It's not designed to shock or dismay the readers, just entertain. I wrote the dialogue my why and used the language (good and bad) the way "I" personally would say it, in an effort to, hopefully, be more entertaining to the people who are good and interested enough to read it. Thank You. (No... Really!!!...I mean it!)

PREFACE

I just hope I've got enough fuckin paper ta finish dis damn book.

Someone very close, who knew me since childhood and for most of my life, told me I should write a book. He knew me well and that I really did the things I'm finally telling about. Most of which I had to keep secret from most people including my own family till now; Even my now ex-wives. That wasn't all that difficult to do, since I was constantly on the move like a gypsy, all over the state, country and continents. He said I was not like most other people. I did so much more than most, and often at the same time, because I had no fear of change, loss or death. Neither money nor the loss of it was ever really a contributing factor as it is to most. He was right. Others called me "unstable". To me, others are afraid to do what they want, or should, for fear of failing, losing money or appearing "unstable" to others. They must live in the norm, as most others do. If this book is a success, not that I really give a flying shit, I'm 79, use to living on nothing and I'll be dead soon anyway (should've been a long time ago), there may be follow ups. But who'da hell knows? Or cares? I'm just telling what I did; the way I did it; to whom and why I did it, in my own bad language, grammar, slang and words. Good or bad, I don't want anyone to change it. I really only wrote it for me anyway, before I forget it all! Never thought I'd live even half this long doing the things I did and places I went. Many of the people I did them with, my friends and partners are long gone now. Even my lifelong friend who said, "Tony, you should write a book!" Many times I've wished I was with them or it was me that didn't make it this far instead of them. I really miss my friends and colleagues. They were all good trustworthy men; rare these days. The beginning chapters, from my childhood, and youth are so different from my later exploits (Wow, I've never used the word "exploits" before in my 79 years)! They're just happy amusing things that happened to me way back then and contributed to my crazy, adventurous life; ... ESPECIALY the one at the drive-in. (Wish I could repeat that one now! Butt I'd probably die ... smiling)!

I sincerely hope that anyone who does read it enjoys the situations I happened into, both on purpose or unintentionally. I loved and enjoyed living thru it all. I have many more true adventures to tell ... if I live long enough. I participated in 23 mercenary missions, with a terrific team of good men, in four different Central American countries for my good hearted Canadian employer. He loved and protected his people ... and so did we. At one time or another all my partners in these jobs/adventures admitted, they would've done it for free, when they saw the misery those poor people suffered in those places.

There are chapters in this book that would be extremely upsetting to some people. Especially to those opinionated individuals who only see things thru their own eyes and live in their own little sheltered world, always quick to judge others and their deeds, but do nothing themselves. They shouldn't read it. From what my friends and family, who have read it told me, it's funny and very interesting. However, there is one particular mercenary chapter that is pretty nasty. Too bad, for what they did, it should have been much worse! I hope who does read it enjoys it and makes a sincere effort to understand the brutal situations. Again, it's not for everyone. I wrote it for me and ... I did it myyyyy wayyyyyyyy!!!

Butt Grandma ... I Wanna Be a *Proctologist* When I Grow Up!

There're so many Assholes around!

Once upon a time, when I was a much younger ... perverted little tyke (I have no clue whatda hell a "tyke" even is ... big or little), of about 4 or 5; my only little friend (nooo ... not da one from "Scarface") Carol Ann, from just 2 houses up da road and I were playing in our dirt driveway. There were no other homes around then and it was a safe, private dirt road. It was a beautiful summer day. After a few different games we decided to try doctor as we had many times before. She was due for her regular checkup, anyway.

It took a while to get through the usual preliminary work, like getting (making), the proper required medical instruments; ... Sticks, not the group; I love'um, but they weren't even born yet! That's probably why I had "Too much time on my hands", back then. I was waiting for them! Hmmmm ... Maybe a couple of nice branches, stiff ... but not too sharp.

Ok, let's open the office for business. Carol's here for her regular examination. She says her tummy hurts. Ok, turn around lift your dress, pull your panties down an bend over... Some things never change! (Even when I grew up! ... Even now!!!)

There's nothing I hate more than being "disturbed" (even though I already really was, even at that tender young age!) in the middle of a serious medical examination. It's so damn unprofessional; even if I didn't know what da hell dat even meant! Here we are standing; Carol Ann bending over holding her knees, dress up, panties at her ankles, in the middle of our dirt driveway (my office ... during regular office hours) with an instrument (stick) stuck in Carol's ... how can I put this ... delicately (and I do mean that literally too)? ... Asshole ... yeah, that'll do it. My face not more than 10 inches away from it. I measured it with the tape measure I always carried even then, for just such occasions; I couldn't read it, but it looked so damn impressive;

when the front door of my home burst open and this crazy old lady; my 85 year old Grandma, whom I loved dearly, even when she was trying ta kill me; burst out screaming in some crazy language. I believe it was Italian (Wappinese). Even at her age she could run, scream, take off her shoes and throw them, accurately, all at the same time! So! That's where Ma learned how ta do dat! Carol took off running in one direction, trying to pull her panties up from her ankles, while I took off in the other. It was like someone yelled "grenade!" That crazy old lady was still screaming so fast and loud in a language we both "normally" understood, but she turned up the speed from thirty three and a third to seventy five RPM (You young people better look up what that means on that damn internet)! Now Carol and I ... her personal physician, met up to re-group in back of the barn (my remote; outta town office). Listening for Grandma (ya know, dat crazy old lady). We were trying to figure out what da hell we did wrong. Naturally, we were only about 5 then, so we didn't actually think in language like "What da <u>hell</u> did we do wrong?" So sweet little Carol Ann asked me "What da fuck got in ta dat crazy oul bitch ... ehy?" I think she had a little Canadian in her ... He would'a hadda be little ... cause she was only ... Never mind...

Anyway, now we're both hiding back there ... in my other office; trembling, trying to figure "Watt" went wrong (I spelt it that way cause we were both so ... "shocked"). Now, probably from nerves, I had ta pee "real bad". Carol Ann too! Butt ... we're not gonna go out dare and "expose ourselves" again ... not dat way anyway. We can do dat right here! Butt, we're not leavin de office! I stand up, open my pants and take ... it out! She's a few feet away; pulls her panties down ... again! (Maybe she should just leave'um off? I think she became a hooker when she grew up). Carol's squatting and peeing. She's watching me ... I'm watching her. Ya know ... I've examined her on many other occasions. Butt, always from the rear... so to speak. Butt, she's facing me now; her eyes glued on my enormous ... Well ... appendage, spouting wee-wee. Now, we totally forgot about Grandma. Carol Ann says

"What's dat?" I said "I don't know", while starring at her ... empty spot. She asked "Can I touch it?" I said "NOOO!! ... You broke yours off already!!!"

Years later, when I returned to my own home town high school, after leaving Catholic grade school; then being ... "<u>Asked </u>to leave" Catholic high school, after my sophomore year (because I tried to punch a priest who slapped me on the ear for no damn reason); I met Carol Ann in the hall. It was so nice to see her again ... from the front. I said "Hi!" Sadly, she had moved to the other side of town, shortly after ... "The Grandma incident" (she probably went to different doctor too). She just nodded her head ... and snubbed me!! ... I couldn't fuckin believe it!!

All those years later ... and she still had a stick up her ass for me!!!
****

*A true story by: Tony Fuckin Z (all except for the punch line, I added later ...... when I was 6)

Long, Long Ago ...... In a Drive-In ...... Far, Far Away
.... *Teen Whores!*

When I was a young lad of 19 years (not a little tyke like da last story), an event occurred in my life that changed it forever (OK, maybe a couple-a days). I'm gonna tell you a story about Mary Lou ... She was the kind of a woman make a ... zombie outta you; along with her pretty little helpers Linda, Rosie, Marie and Anny. I'm telling you about it now, and even though I lived it, (and I do mean lived it) I still have trouble believing it ever really happened ... to ME! I wish ta hell it would again ... No ... Really I do ... Even if I don't live thru it this time.

I was trolling for female type personnel one beautiful Saturday evening in almost-semi- acceptable, down town Hasting-on-Hudson, New York, with plans to find myself a pretty young female gendered type, to take to the Elmsford drive-in, for a pleasant evening of snacking and movie watching. At least that's what I planned on telling her (I was really planning on snacking <u>on</u> her; if she was willing). Back then it was a great and affordable way to spend a Friday or Saturday night; or both. I was, slowly driving thru town by the local corner pizza parlor in my "chick-mobile"; a sparkling white 54 mercury coupe with a bright orange top, rear skirts, glass pack mufflers and stolen 57 Cadillac hub caps (I know they were stolen, because I stole them myself in the Dobbs Ferry Hospital parking lot one night!), and white, real leather bench seats; all irresistible to teenage girls in those days. Every time I'd pass thru town all the chicks would smile and wave. It's great to be 19 ... and brainless. Like most guys my age I only had one thing on my mind (what little of it there was). And it wasn't other guys ... or safe driving.

This one particular evening I spotted someone I had my eye on for quite a while (both in fact). We'll call her ... Linda ... cause dat was her name. I'd been trying to single her out for a while, but whenever I saw her she always had the same small group around her, like a pack. I was kind of like a cheetah trying to single out a gazelle from the herd ... for consumption. An I do mean dat literally to! I never really knew Linda except by sight and that was more than enough. Eventually, I started calling the group "Linda's pack". Later I found out she really was "The leader of the pack".

This particular evening though, Linda was standing in front of the local pizza place ... alone. This is my shot! Linda was almost my height, big brown eyes, with looonnnggg chestnut hair, my favorite, all the way down her back (none on her head; just down her back! ... Sorry ... I hadda) perfect body, beautiful ... head to toe ... HOT!! The girls in her pack were much more then "mildly tepid" themselves, but there were always at least 4 or 5 together. What da hell am I gonna do wit all dem, he asked himself; spelling all da words incorrectly ... in his head? Ya know what I'm saying here? Too damn bad if you don't. Besides I'm gonna show you how wrong an adorable an innocent, young child, like myself, can be. I thought ... nuttin could possibly go wrong. So I pulled over to the curb and said, "Hey Lin, whatta ya doin?" (Classy, eh?) Lin walks over, leans down and sticks her beautiful head into the passenger window. Fortunately for her... it was open; brushing her gorgeous hair from her equally gorgeous face. Her smile along with her huge brown eyes already sent me to another galaxy, but I was cool; on the outside. I love big brown eyes ... big blue eyes ... big green eyes ... and excessively large hazel eyes (I didn't wanna be too fuckin redundant, over, an over an over an over again); but mostly, big brown eyes. One time I dated a great 18 year old, platinum blond Go-Go girl, from Beacon NY, named Debbie. She had one blue an one brown eye. I guess in case I couldn't make up my mind which I loved more.

I said, "I'm thinkin about going to the Elmsford Drive-In; wanna go?" She says "Yeah, hang on a minute I'll be right back." She went back into the pizza place. A couple-a minutes later she came back out, leaned in and said, "Can we take a couple of my friends with us?" Just then I moved my foot and felt a really sharp, nasty pain in my chest. That's when I realized my heart had dropped to the floor and I was kicking it. I thought to myself, Oh ... Whoopy Shits! A Saturday night; shot ta hell ... "OK! Gettum!" Grumbling to myself, as I watched that incredibly perfect butt wiggling away (XX*XX! XX*XX, I can't say what else I was thinking about it. I got _way_ too much fuckin class fadat shit). It was the first time I ever even talked to her, so I consoled myself thinking, at least "I got in" almost ... so to speak (wink, wink). OK, here they come; one, two, three, four, five!!!!! Good thing this car's got bench seats and a lotta room or I'd be screwed! (Naaahhh; it's too fuckin soon fadat one; maybe later?) I've got three in the back, two in the front. At least I've got Linda's deliciously perfect butt snuggling up against me. (Ehhy, ... how'd jew like me goin out wit chour daughta???)

Back then there were some great deals. The drive-in charged by the car load, not the number of individuals. I paid a whole five bucks for all 6 of us ... and the car!

OK, we're here. Let's all get ready to watch a movie now with Linda, Mary Lou, Marie, Anny and Rosie ... in order of importance ... to me. I was trying to see the good side (not that I actually had one). All of them were above average in female "attracti-ousity" on any given day (butt I had no idea just how much givin there would be on this particular night). The least, Rosie was a 7+. Linda and Mary Lou were 9's in anybody's book. Again, maybe I could single them out from the pack at different times in the future. It's amazing what teenage hormones will do to a young man's head ... s. It's disgusting! Annnd so am I!!! This may be a God-send. Although I don't think "He" would have approved of my plans!

I bring the speaker in and set it on the window. Now everyone's getting comfortably settled. Rosie's by the door in the passenger seat; she opens the glove compartment. I don't know why. Girls just do things because they know we want them ... and we won't beat them ... that much! She squeals "Wow! Booze!!" I was nineteen. In those days the drinking age in NY was only eighteen, as were most of these girls. It was also still legal to carry liqueur in the vehicle; open or not. She found my crown shaped bottle of Crown Royal Canadian whiskey ... ehy. I, being the suave, debonair, man about town, type, also always had a cooler in the trunk with a bag of ice cubes on weekend nights like this; paper cups, chilled champagne glasses, chilled, cheap, four bucks a bottle NYS Champagne (in a wet towel, of course ... What'a my ... a savage?), ginger ale and a box of goodies including cherries, olives, toothpicks, popcorn, pretzels, chips and whatever da hell else I thought would make girls happy (and then they would make me happy too). I remember that old song, Maaake someone happy, maaake just ... someone happy and they will make yooou happy tooooooooooooooooooooooo.

When they saw what I had they squealed with delight (which I wished they would also do later, if they saw what other treats I had for them. But that was just wishful thinking). We popped and poured the Champagne for everyone. All the girls said they'd never had it before so I told them they could finish it. I hate Champagne! Butt we made a nice toast ... I love toast! Especially when it's to a beautiful female butt (dats my secret, French toast)! Everyone was having a good time. When the Champagne ran out we were already nibbling at the chips and pretzels so we started making mixed drinks and doing shots. Nobody gave a damn about the movie. I don't even remember what da hell it was. I didn't care then; I don't care now, so why the hell did I even bring it up? Linda wanted me to sit in the middle. I said, "OK". Those older cars had no headrests and the seats were big and real comfortable. I kept catching Linda looking back at the girls in the back with a sly look in her eye. I always figured her to be the pack leader. I was never a "big breast man" but I never had anything against them (OK, my face a few times). She filled out the pink blouse she was wearing very nicely; it looked like she was trying to poke two holes in it. But it must've been too tight because she opened a few buttons; then gave me a look I knew only too well. I was looking right into those big beautiful brown eyes. Uh-oh, I think I see ... the devil in there; he's a she!!! From the corner of my right eye I saw Rosie doing the same to her blouse. Hmmm, dat booze loosened me up a lot. Apparently, it's not just me (Oh golly wiz! Mama never said there'd be days like this!). I'm a sinner... I can live with that! But maybe not thru tonight! And if I don't, whodafuck cares! There's worse ways ta die. Linda glanced again to the girls in back, then grabbed my face and planted a kiss on my lips; jamming her tongue down my throat. I believe she was licking my tonsils (I kept mine. Ta hell wit da damn ice cream. They only had chocolate. I don't like chocolate!). I could feel Rosie unbutton my shirt; rip it open and start licking my nipple. Whodahells wet tongue is that in my right ear, another one's in the left! Who'da hell cares whose it is! Just don't stop ... please! Now Rosie slid down to the floor. Some other wonderful angel / devil, whatever, has leaned over the seat and taken over my right nipple. It's all yours baby! I got another one over... oooh God ... or... whoever? Linda's on that one now! Rosie!? Are you checking to see if I remembered to zip up my ... Oooh! ... Gooood girl ... Well, maybe not "Good"... per se. Thanks soooo much for checking on that for me! Oh ...Yeah!!! Make sure it's ... I wouldn't want you to just give it "lip service". And to think ... I was gonna go tada snack bar and buy them all hot dogs. They seem to like hot Italian sausage much better! Linda just took off her bra ... AND Jeans!!! Apparently she needs to check on Rosie's work ... it's always nice when friends share. This is the best "blow by blow" description I've ever given ... or had! Who'da hell's grabbin my face from the back seat? Different tongue, I hope she brushed. This could be "unsanitary"! Those two are taking off my jeans. Oh! ... Those little scamps! Holy shit! Did I die and go ta fuckin heaven? Literally? Nhhhh ... I don't think they let you in for shit like this (I'm glad I'm not still an altar boy or I might be doin dis wit da priests!) Hey ... They started it! I'm just an innocent young victim here. OK, OK ... a victim ... we'll skip that innocent bull shit! But, I feel so cheap and ... used! Please! Do it MORE ... I love feeling that way! Rosie's climbing into the back seat. Maybe cause

Linda took her sausage? Someone else's cumming up front (I think it's me). I can't tell who yet because she stuck her beautiful butt in my face while she was doing it! I'm glad she hung there awhile. It was delicious. I love rump roast. Maybe that's why she straddled the seat in that awkward position so long? Mary Lou apparently has a taste for hot Italian sausage too. I hope Linda's gonna share it with her... Oh Linda ... how thoughtful. I've got a tongue in my ear and another on my nipple. I think my brain's exploding ... among other things. Now Linda's squatting on my lap; I wonder what she's gonna ... Oh ... dat! She grabbed Mary Lou's hair an pulled her over to lick her nipples! She seemed happy to comply. What da hell did I do ta deserve dis? Whatever it was, I gotta do it again ... a lot. They're nuts! Now they're trying to pull me into the back seat. OK, I'll help. None of them have pants on anymore ... or panties ... or bras! I gotta get more of that fuckin champagne; maybe a couple-a cases (and that's a real accurate description of that champagne too). I'm on my back now, in the back seat (maybe dat's why they call it dat), there's a beautiful 17 year old butt parked on my face. Legs, breasts, asses and those other tasty wet snacks everywhere (I could use some nylon here though ... Some guys are never satisfied ... Well...). My face on one, my hands on another! I don't know what belongs ta who, or care, so I'm lickin'um ALL; just in case! They're going back and forth over the seat sharing the meal; sometimes sitting on it ... and feeding me ... everything they had on the menu! I don't know how nutritious, butt I must say, EVERYTHING was scrumptious! Butts too! All I can eat for five bucks, now that's a real deal. Best meal I ever had, and the portions were amazing; hot, juicy, tender. They REALLY know how da put out a <u>spread</u>! They also seemed to love that hot Italian sausage. I should've been a fuckin food critic (literally). This wonderful dining experience went on for at least an hour and a half-plus. We'd slow down for a breather, a drink now and then; then start again when someone wanted dessert. Like a hard young nipple or when Anny bent over the seat in front of me with her magnificent, young ass in my face and said how-bout some dessert? (I'm not worrying about calories tonight) I spanked those beautiful cheeks a few times to warm them up; then buried my face between them; jamming my tongue into that adorable little pucker as deep as I could. While that was happening, Marie seemed to want another helping of hot Italian sausage. Thank God for "leftovers"! During all this ... "stuff", I witnessed for the first time in my young life, girl on girl. It's good for them to have a varied diet; especially, when I'm watching. When there was no room for everyone to get at me, a few times, in their frenzied heat, they started licking and massaging one another's breasts among other things; including all those other things!

Talk about things that'll make ya crazy; at one time, during a short "recess", I peeked over into the front seat. There seemed to be some activity up there. Linda was in a "numeric" position with Mary Lou. Wonderfully disgusting! Or disgustingly wonderful! I can see why Lin was the leader of the pack. They all seemed to follow her lead or instructions. Let's try that back here ladies (a very loose use of that particular term). I didn't have to ask twice. Rosie and Marie jumped right into it on the seat (like they'd done it many times before) while Anny half stood up sticking her hot young butt in my face ... again (she really liked doing that; I guess I'll just have to put up with it) and said "Spank me again". I couldn't hurt her feelings, so I did ... spank her I mean. Then I kissed and licked each cheek "to make them all better". I don't know which of us loved it more? I peeked up and realized she was leaning over da seat and licking the ass cheeks of one of the girls in the front seat too. Then, of course, I buried my face in the most obvious place and made a pig of myself (like that took a lotta effort; oink, oink) with that tasty treat in front of me (no wonder my Mom nicknamed me "Uh Puerco," <u>the Pig</u>). Her hot red cheeks wrapped around my face spurring my tongue to go nuts (I think it even got hard)! I was holding onto her beautiful thighs, pulling myself in harder to get every last bit of that delicious dessert (Ma also taught me <u>never to waste food</u>). I could hear moan after moan cumming from the front seat and there was quite a bit in the back now too. It was the craziest, and one of the most wonderful, nights of my life. I remember it so clearly; it's like I'm still there (I wish da fuck I was; and I mean <u>that</u> literally too). I did my best to make them all happy. My Pop taught me "The women always come first". Although ... I don't think he meant it in exactly the same way; butt I've always made it my priority, especially in this way. And in the future it served me very well ... an dem too! Unfortunately, it never happened again. I never had more than two girls at a time after that (not dat I'm complaining about dat either). Shortly after, I met my now beautiful ex-wife. Same age as them and she knew them all from high school, so we kept our distance. Damn it! I should-a stayed with dem! She never knew about it, as far as I know. I don't know what da hell got into those girls that night ... well ... besides me I mean. I wanted to do it again; every weekend! Both nights! I'll take a lotta Vit. E!!!

The ride home was interesting too. They put some of their clothes back on ... damnit! It was a warm summer night. The car windows were all open; about midnight. The songs of the day were mostly the Beetles and Dave Clark Five (early 60's, British invasion). We were all still a little high (you know when your mouth is dry you're plenty high ... words of wisdom from the wonderful George Thorogood). As we passed thru each town on our way back to Hastings, they stuck their adorable heads out all the windows singing along ... loud! The radio was blaring, but they were changing all da words. I was expecting to get pulled over, but fortunately, no crooked, slimy, greasy palmed, town cops saw or heard us. In Ardsley it was "She loves it, yeah, yeah, yeah ... She loves it yeah, yeah, yeah ... and with a dick like his ... ya know she shooould ... be glad ... yeah, yeah, yeah ... Yeah, yeah, yeah, yeaaaah!"

Thru Dobbs Ferry it was the DC-5 with "You say that you love it ... all of the time. You say that you need it ... it'll always be mine ... and I'm feeling ... Gladis all over... yeah am'a feelin ... Gladis all over, so glad its maaaaiyne. I'll make it happy, they'll never be blue. You'll have no trouble … cause I'll only suck you … The entire fuckin ride! (A perfect description)!

Next morning, I wake up from this incredible dream, half thinking, I was drinking … too much; and that's all it was. I was just half loaded and that it didn't really happen … or … did it? When I try to stand up I feel like someone just kneed me … a couple-a times. Males only have so much to give. They kept trying to get more! I lost count how many times, but I still kept trying. (My boys kept trying to accommodate; like my Pop said!) I got dressed and limped out to my Merc. On the front floor, pink panties; Linda's! On the back floor, white ones'! … Who knows? I'm sure Linda wasn't wearing two pairs. OMG! (No; I don't think He's speaking to me right now)! It wasn't a fuckin dream!!! (Well … in some ways … it was.) Now I'm thinking, maybe I can use returning the panties as an excuse for a return engagement … Hmmmm?

Yeah, that Mary Lou an Linda an Rosie an Anny an Marie made a zombie outta me … for days! My "equipment" ached for three days + … butt I never complained. I limped around in a "fuckin daze"… for… fuckin days! Like a zombie! An incredibly Happy, Smiling, Fuckin Zombie!

Ya know … I should-a got a fuckin "<u>Bachelor's Degree</u>" fadat!… I really miss them too! *******

* <u>Happily</u> and <u>literally</u>, a true fuckin story … with a blow by blow description, by: Tony Fuckin Z *

The Beginning: High School Confidential ... *Real Confidential!*

My high school years were slightly different than most kids. In 1960 I was a sophomore in high school and a punk (OK, OK, devastatingly handsome; but still ... a punk!), but a very patriotic and political, handsome punk. The idea of Fidel Castro really pissed me off. Of course, like most people, I really knew nothing about anything, but I still had an opinion about everything; again ... like most stupid people. In my later years I realized with all his faults, and there were plenty, he was better then what they already had, but still no fuckin good for Cuba; and I hate communism and dictatorships! However, I thought it was up to me personally to get rid of him! While I was growing up, or at least attempting to, my Pop used to take me to an old Cuban barber and his son, just off Getty Square in Yonkers, New York. The son had a son my age that I played with whenever we went there and we became good friends. One day, when I was about sixteen, I decided to get involved so, I called him up from a pay phone and asked if he knew a Cuban rebel group he could get me in touch with. He did, so I told him not to use my real name. He never knew where I lived anyway, we were always at his place; it was perfect and it worked.

The group was small, only ten students; seven Cubans and three Americans plus the two ex-Special Forces instructors (77th Airborne) and one anti-Castro Cuban exile made up the group of thirteen. It was like a damn spy movie. They picked us up in a van with no windows, four nights a week at pre-designated times and locations that changed periodically. I went to the next town, Hastings, for my pickup so no one would know where I lived ... just in case. We rode for about a half hour to some big estate, I don't know whose but I always thought it was in North Tarrytown, or Ossining NY, because of its seeming vastness (we fired many weapons there and no one ever bothered us) and the time it took to get there. Most of the training was at night but some weekend days. We learned so much (Like, the first rule in guerrilla warfare is, cut off their supply of bananas!), improvised explosives and weapons, booby traps, jungle combat tactics an techniques, weapons operation, survival, knife fighting, guard elimination, camouflage, tank destruction an capture, building demolition, guerrilla warfare, night warfare etc., etc. I loved every second of it. I soaked up as much as I could, but in those days I was the smallest guy there. One of the green berets told me I was a "tough little shit". I was only about a hundred an fifteen pounds then, (Although, that's heavy for a turd ... even a tough one!) so I'd better build up and learn some kind of martial art in case I had to fight with my hands. I didn't even know what the hell a martial art was back then. Except for Judo, they weren't popular in this country yet. Anyway, I found a school in White Plains, New York; I joined the judo / Jujitsu class but when I stayed one night to watch the karate class I decided to take both; in those days it was only six bucks a week; five each, if you took more than one art. Later, I also joined the aikido class, taught by the same Japanese jujitsu sensei. When I eventually started to understand the three, while getting better at them, I began mixing aspects of all three at the advice of my, then karate sensei, who also was a green beret. He wasn't into strict "art form" or tradition, but believed in practical fighting and defense. He was from the deep Bronx and had a lot of real, street fighting experiences. He was also the only guy who ever knocked me out! Sensei Rios said to blend the best of all three arts, adding weapons and the concepts of guerrilla warfare into my fighting; so I always have. That was the real birth of Kyokuninjakan karate; My System. Later, I used the martial arts training nights to cover the mercenary training nights. It was perfect; my family, or girlfriend, never really knew where the hell I was. Sometimes, even I got confused!

A problem came up when the berets told us that a semi-large group was planning an invasion in the spring of 1961, on a day that Castro took over or some other dumbass, symbolic bullshit. He said the U.S. (JFK) said it would not back the assault and they were also not trained enough or well enough equipped. I don't know where they got their info, but I always thought they were "Fuckin CIA" (Dogs of War). They told us not to go this trip because the assault was destined to fail and it was a waste of lives that would accomplish nothing. Some of us were fine with that, because we knew they knew what the hell they were talking about. However, it did not sit well with a few / most of the Cubans. They said we should go anyway and be "martyrs" for Cuba. I said if I died fighting for freedom and democracy that was one thing; but to die for some stupid martyr bullshit was out. And besides, I wasn't even Cuban! If they want to be martyrs, they can go ahead. I'll wait till the real fight starts and we at least have a chance of winning. The Cubans were enraged at us three Americans, and especially at the berets, who said we three made the right choice. About six weeks later the Bay of Pigs fiasco happened; the berets were right on the money and probably saved our lives. The Cubans, however, didn't see it that way. I think they felt betrayed. I always wondered why they didn't go. But we didn't know that yet. It must have been the exile that brought them back because, as far as we knew, no one but the three instructors knew where the training camp was. They hadn't shown up for the next few training sessions, after the fiasco news, but we kept training. Two of us were sent out on an objective mission one night, Leo stayed behind with the berets. We were always taught to return quietly and cautiously, even to our own camp. Or hide and watch, in case the camp was compromised and a trap was waiting. There were two of the Cubans out in front of the shed; odd since they hadn't been to training, or picked up by the van with us that night. We approached the back of the shed like two cats (not pussies; cats). Through the cracks in the boards we could see inside and hear what was being said. There were five armed Cubans inside and the exile was talking in a "not too" friendly voice. The two berets and Leo were kneeling with their hands behind their heads facing the wall. We didn't know where the seventh Cuban was and it worried us. The exile was saying how they had been betrayed by the Americans, "again!" But this time they weren't going to get away with it. They were waiting for us to come back; that's why they posted the two guards out front. I guess they didn't figure us coming in the back door (that's always been my favorite). At least we had some time for a quick plan since they were waiting for our return. We needed to deal with the guards quietly first, but we were worried about that missing Cube. Where da-hell was he? We had to chance it. It looked like they were working up to a triple execution. We moved around both sides of the shed. The sentries were at both ends about twenty feet apart; that made it perfect as long as we could take them out simultaneously ... Or, at the same time ... whichever came first! ... Quietly! I could see, Stan, in the dark across from me so I hand singled him to move first, so I could follow instantly. A micro second after he sprang, I did too. We used something they taught us called "scrambled eggs". A totally silent, instant kill; grab the face from the back around neck, gaging the mouth and pulling the head back and to one side, then shoving a knife up into the base of the skull, into the brain from the rear, an twisting it.

They said it was painless, but ... how da hell could they know? I hadn't learned to break necks yet. Now comes the hard part. Take out five more quickly, without losing anyone in a big sloppy shootout; or getting killed! Sometimes it pays to be the little guy; he's harder to hit! Stan kicked the door open; Freddie and I dove in, rolled on the floor and everything went nuts for a few seconds. The berets and Leo dropped to the deck, face first. Freddie was in semi-auto, so I could control shooting the shocked, standing targets that were on both sides of me, without hitting any of my own. It sounded like the 4th of July in there for a few seconds, but I was rolling around and firing until all five were down; Stan also chimed in a lot with his carbine from the open door, adding to their confusion. Guards and all; It all happened in less than 2 minutes. Our people were safe, but we never knew what happened to the seventh Cuban. We eventually just figured he wouldn't go along with them; or they killed him. Leo and the two berets seemed quite glad to see us and, laughing, said we passed our mission test for that night. Stan asked the instructors what we should do with them. One of the berets said "You've done enough. We'll just get you guys home; relax, and we'll clean things up here". I couldn't believe how calm I was during the whole damn thing. I wasn't nervous or shaking; even after. One beret commented to Stan, who was shaking like a leaf and stammering. He said that it was normal; especially in his first real action. I wasn't. I was completely calm and felt perfectly normal. That's when I realized I was made for this shit. The other beret even smiled and said so. It all came so easy, natural, as though I'd done it a thousand times before. I worried about the missing Cuban, but I still felt no fear, as if I was ... invincible. "Invinciousity" is the best policy in applications like this! There would be many more similar episodes to come, but that night was Freddie's first six notches. **

*After thought: Many years later, one of my very best and trusted "Outlaw" friends, Big Ray, with whom I had many adventures, asked me if I had ever "Smoked a Cuban?" At that time he was making great money smuggling and selling Cuban cigars into the US from Canada. He sold them to rich stock brokers, at the illegal, hi stakes card games he through, at his private men's club in Poughkeepsie, New York. I remember laughing when I answered "Yeah, I smoked a bunch ... and I love their cigars too". He laughed, but I know he didn't know or understand why, because I never told him or anyone else about that night.

Canada One ... *No! ...They Didn't!!*

In 1973, I was living in my own private paradise. A-frame house on the backside of a beautiful Adirondack lake; three acres of my own secluded wilderness two hundred yards off a dirt road, only two hundred feet outside the Adirondack Park border markers. I had one mile of virgin forest on one side (no virgins inside) and a half mile of woods to the next cottage on the other. Fireplace, deck, well, beach and dock; no Goddamn lawn to cut; all surrounded by miles of nothing but magnificent wilderness, twenty five miles deep across the road. Black bears by the front door, deer at the back and fish in the lake. I was right where I belonged. Mornings I'd awaken to the beautiful sound of loons or flocks of Canada geese on the lower Chateaugay Lake. My karate school in beautiful downtown Malone, NY was doing OK. There were a few loons there too. I spent my "spare time" protecting good people, working as a mercenary in Central America for a very kind, Canadian plantation owner; fighting forest fires with my friend/student, Don, the local forest ranger, teaching hand to hand combat at Dannemora maximum security state prison (to the guards; not the prisoners); being a personal body guard or as a womanizing pig. And not necessarily in that order! (Ya know ... I <u>really do</u> miss <u>dat</u> place). I also, occasionally worked as a bouncer in a number of local discos and bars that featured live rock & roll band entertainment on weekends. I've always been the multitask guy ... I like ta screw up a lotta stuff at the same time. I get bored easily; especially when no one's tryin na kill me; like now. That's why I'm writing this. It'll keep me busy till someone else tries. There were a lot of great people up there but naturally there's always some "brainless shit kickers" that can't leave other people alone. Their entertainment was getting drunk or stoned on weekends and starting fights with people who just wanted to have a good time, peacefully, after a long work week. That's when the owners would call my school asking for a couple of clean-up nights from myself or one of the higher ranking students; usually Larry. He was big, great shape, only twenty one and familiar with all the local dance spots. I became friends with the guys in a great three piece band, "Frozen Sunshine." They played for my back yard beach party, from my deck, under the multi-colored flood lights, I installed just for them. They were fantastic! They played most popular rock and roll songs better than the originals. (The originals were another band; but they really sucked!)

Anyway, after one great, Sunday night party (they could only play on none-paying gig nights), everyone had left and gone back to town.

Malone was twenty three miles away, in those days. It probably still is; it'd be way too expensive to move it. It was about 1:30 AM and non-typically after a party, I was alone. As I started cleaning up, I heard a small noise coming from the spare bedroom. I knew it wasn't Gonia, my cat; she was on the couch ... tired from all the dancing. When I opened the door to check it out (and possibly kill whoever it was), on the double bed was a beautiful young thing. Fortunately for me ... it was a girl! I have nothing against gays (and I mean that literally too) but I'm a one trick pony; and girls are my trick ... so to speak. She was sitting in the center of the bed with nothing on but a lacy white bra and bikini panties. What made it worse ... or better, depending on how you look at it; and I looked ... very hard! (That one's all yours) I'd put black light bulbs in, all over the house, because I tacked crazy day glow posters up for the party. Her bra and panties were glowing, as were her pretty white teeth. She had beautiful silky, long chestnut brown hair flowing over her breasts (none on her head; just on her breasts! It was disgusting!!) No! Really! In short ... or long, she was HOT! I said "I don't know who you are (and at that point, I really didn't care) but everyone else has gone. Who brought you?" She said she just got a ride out from Malone, when she heard there was a party out here. I said "butt (nooo ... it's not a misprint,) how'da hell are you gonna get home ta night?" I'd have driven her if she needed me to (Maybe, I'll drive her later... if she's in the mood). She said she had no home to go back to; she was on the road and out of money. Her name was Leslie. Leslie asked if she could stay with me for the night and she'd find her own way back to town in the morning. I said "No! You can stay till you get back on your feet" (Noooo ... I didn't mean just in the morning. Stop thinking like a disgusting pervert ... that's my job). Young girls shouldn't be traveling alone like she was. There's too many guys like me around! But unlike most, I'd never take advantage or do anything to hurt her. I knew she'd be absolutely safe with me, so I said "Now go to sleep, we'll have breakfast and talk about it in the morning".

I closed everything up, including her bedroom door. Put some wood in the fireplace and got into my queen size, pull out convertible, right in front of it. On my other side, it was all thermal pane glass facing the deck, so I could see the beautiful lake and full moon; and become a werewolf, if I so desired. But right now, I was a different kind of wolf and desired something else. However, I'm not low enough to require sex or money from a poor young girl alone, helpless and down on her luck. Or any female! That's pure "Slime" (I'm just impure, but I'm not slime)! So, I just got all comfy and cuddled up with my teddy bear, Baby Bartholomew ...... (<u>Don't</u>!!!), when I heard her door open. I figured she had ta wee-wee or something. A few seconds later I felt her pulling back the covers (at least I was hoping it was her; there were a lotta black bears in my neighborhood) and climb into bed in back of me. I said "Leslie, I said there's no need for this. You don't have to pay me in any way to stay here". In a soft, sweet voice, she asked "Can I; ... If I want to?? Cause I really do." Then she gave me a looonnng, loving kiss ... Whew! OK! I guess I'll just <u>have</u> ta do dis; ya know ... just to make her feel welcome and safe. The things I have to put up with for the sake of others. Sometimes ya just gotta take one fada team. When is it all gonna end? (Not too damn soon, I hope). Man, did that girl have some energy! In the immortal words of Rosanne Rosanna Danna "Ah taught Ah was gonna daa".

In the morning when we got up (she only let me sleep about 2 hours), I made us my normal breakfast ... corn flakes and tripe. Oddly, Leslie didn't seem very hungry; said she'd be happy with just coffee, eggs and toast; said "I'll skip the tripe today, thank you". Go figga?

There's nothing like hot, boiled cow stomach with a side of corn flakes and milk, to get the day going. Leslie poured about half a bottle of catsup ...... on everything! Even her toast! She was addicted to it! After we ate ... and I added "giant bottles of catsup" to my grocery list, we sat down and started talking about her situation, for about an hour or so, when she, nonchalantly, tells me ... she's fifteen years old!

FIFTEEN!!! Damn it! She could-a been a little more chalant!!! Even I draw the line at sixteen .... most of the time! Did it occur to you to let me know that before I, unwittingly, committed a felony! No!! Multiple felonies! At least six! In every possible physical configuration!! Numerically and otherwise!!! There'll be no more of that bullshit! What da hell's wrong with you "little girl"? If I touch that pretty bare ass of yours again, it'll be ta spank it for being so damn dumb! From now on, you sleep in the spare room where I put you last night ... and stay in there!!!... I'll sleep out here ... ALONE!!! ... Occasionally.

Leslie looked, talked and had the body and legs of a fully developed, Hot, nineteen or twenty year old girl. In other words, trouble! I asked why she was on the move. She told me her dad came back from Viet Nam and became a minister, after suffering deep psychological trauma there. Then he molested her when she was thirteen, after her mother divorced him and moved to Arizona (obviously, he wasn't a Catholic priest; they only molest boys). What a fuckin mess for this poor little girl. Anyway, I said the rule stands (standing was something I was having trouble with after a night with her); and that goes for anyone else who tries ta lay a hand, or what-ever else, on her. Yeah, I know! Once the loaf's open, nobody misses a slice. This was gonna be tough! Leslie was HOT and dumb; the normal dumb innocents of a fifteen year old, with the body and legs of a model. A real pain in the ass; which is exactly what she'll get if I have any more problems with her! But Ruby Begonia, my cat, liked her, and that was <u>really</u> rare. Normally, she only liked me ... and Sarah ... her gynecologist. If I just let her go, who knows what might happen to her (Leslie ... not Begonia)? Maybe she'll become a hooker or get raped, even killed (again; Leslie ... not Begonia). I can't do it. And I still have my quiet "sudden excursions" to Central America to deal with. I needed to enlist my good friend / student Larry, ta help. We had each other's backs most of the time. I made her give me her dad's phone number so I could at least let him know she was safe, cared for and not buried in the woods somewhere; promising not to tell him where she was. He seriously fucked up, but that didn't mean he didn't love his kid. War can do nasty things to people's heads (I was fortunate enough not to need it ... I got fucked up without it). My simple life's getting real complicated. And so, as Oliver Hardy used to say "Well ... Here's another fine mess you got me into!" But I had no idea how big or dangerous it would be. Or that it would involve local border drug smugglers and dealers in Malone and Plattsburg, NY. I really never expected it to involve "Canada One"; then the biggest coast to coast biker gang in all of Canada! I hate biker gangs! As well as drug dealers! I soon found out Leslie had a real talent for, unintentionally, getting herself into a pile of shit ... and dragging me in with her!

Most days I brought Leslie with me to my karate school in the center of Malone, so I could keep an eye on her. Larry helped me with that. She straightened up the office; cleaned the school and hung out. I also taught her some nasty self-defense before regular classes started. Then I let her go down into town for a while. Big mistake!!! It seemed OK for a week or so, but one day she came back an asked me if she could buy some different clothes. She only had the tight jeans and sweater she showed up with. On her travels, another girl she met, in a similar situation, had taken off with her pack and clothes. I said "Yeah, I've been trying to put some cash together for that". The other guys on my merc team and I kept spending most of our money bringing food and things back for the kids in the "off plantation" Central American villages, on our return missions. So cash wise, things were always lean. A couple of days later I gave her forty bucks to get some new clothes. Things were not as expensive back then, and it was even cheaper to live up there; especially at AME's department and grocery store. She told me she saw some clothes there she really liked. When she got the money she was happy as a clam, (clams are always smiling) and thanked me with a big hug and kiss ... on the cheek this time. I had no idea what she was buying. Later, she came back to the school wearing the shortest mini dress I've ever seen; just about 2 inches below her perfect butt cheeks. Also wearing new, very high heel shoes and sheer pantyhose ... that's it! Nothing else! Not even panties! I found that out when she turned around, bent over and flashed me her perfect ass, in my office! She had her jeans, shirt, sneakers, underwear etc. in a big bag. I said "Whatda!?!? Did ya decide to become the first street walker in Malone? That's not a dress; it's a t-shirt! She told me she blew the whole forty bucks on that trouble making outfit. I said "You walk around like that and that's not the only thing you'll be blowin ... for forty bucks!" You're making me nuts little girl! At that point I locked the school door; grabbed her wrist, pulled her back into the office; closed that door too. I said "It's about time my palm and your pretty ass had a heated conversation". I put her over my lap; obviously, no need to pull up her dress, and began to spank her pantyhose covered ass for a good five minutes. All the while, explaining why she couldn't do things like this. Then I peeled down the sheer pantyhose, not like they actually hid anything; butt for the purely psychological effect, while she kicked, squealed and struggled; then I through in an additional bonus ten minutes or so. When I finally let her up, she stood in front of me bouncing up and down, rubbing her bright red, very deserving butt. I told her from now on, she's gonna dress and act like a fifteen year old, not a hooker; made her change back to her jeans, then gave her another ten bucks and sent her to buy some type of stretch pants to wear with that dress / t-shirt, or I'd double what she already got. I've never believed in hitting small children, at all. My father never hit me, even when I knew I deserved and expected it ...... <u>an I'm Perfect</u>! I love women (and Anchovies; ya know, the curly ones with the little capers in the middle) and I can't / won't slap or harm any woman. Butt, I found when words no longer work and you're pushed to the end of your rope with a female "a good spanking always works". I learned that way back when I was only thirteen, with my first real girlfriend, Mary Ellen; Mary Ellen was fourteen; after that, I nicknamed her "Hot

Cheeks". She loved it! It was something I learned from my older friend and kind of hero/ mentor, Eddie. Eddie was a much older and wiser sixteen; ... and he had a car!! One day when I was hanging out at a local park, where he was with his pretty blond girl friend, Stella (Stellaaaaaaaa!). Eddie was trying to explain something to me. Stella (Stellaaaaaaaa!), his girl, kept interrupting, horsing around and making fun of what he was saying. Eddie grabbed her wrist, pulled her across his lap and began spanking her very cute butt, over her tight little shorts, about twenty or so times. After that, she sat down beside him ... quietly. He said "And remember howda do that too (he gave me his personal recipe for rump roast). It always works! Butt, when you're alone; remove all that damn wrapping, and get to the meat of the matter." Fittingly, it happened in Ghoul Park, in Dobbs Ferry, NY. Ghoul, in Italian, which I am, means "Ass". We always used to say "We go ta Ghoul Park, ta park our ghouls".

As I expected, after that, things quieted down with Leslie for a while. At least till the sting and the em-bare ass-ment wore off. Then one day she didn't come back to the school. I waited till after the last class; no Leslie. I started to panic. I had a painful sick feeling in my gut (nooo ... it wasn't gas!). This is new ... It's 10 PM; and I don't know where my children are!! Larry and I, split up, walking all over town looking for her. No dice ... Or Leslie! It's too bad we didn't have cell phones, back then. I was so worried, I didn't go home. I slept in my office; barely, with the doors unlocked and lights on that night, in case she came back. Next morning, nothing; but about noon, one of my best students, on his lunch minute (Jason was a very fast eater), who knew of my situation with her, stopped in and said he just saw her in front of the local slime pit. The Cripple Creek! It was the town drug den; a real sewer! As in all sewers, it was filled with scumbags and pieces of shit! All the dealers and typical asshole types in town hung out there. Pot heads, coke heads, pill junkies, ya know ... ASSHOLES! Fittingly, it was way down on the only shitty back street in town. The State Police

BCI (then many of my students) had been trying to shut it down for a couple of years according to my friend/student "Chick F." He was the head of the Franklin County State Police BCI, stationed in Malone NY, at the time. I kind-a went a little nuts when he told me where he just saw her. After all we were going through with her already; now this. Who knows where da hell she slept last night; or with who (or what)!? I was already at war with these slime balls since Lee Ann, one of my teenage girl students, told me people from there had been enlisting kids in their early teens to sell pot to eleven and twelve year olds at their school. Lee was only fourteen and they'd approached her and even her younger sister Donna. They hated me at that dump because, through several previous incidents, I made damn sure they knew I was their enemy. I got into Bronc, my camouflaged 66 Bronco and went racing down to pay them a visit; or... visit them and make them pay! There were no vehicles parked in front so, wanting to make an "impression", I drove my camoed Bronco right onto the sidewalk, pointing it nose first, right up against, and blocked the open doorway! Got out, climbed over the hood and down into the open door. Everyone, about twelve of them, scattered to the walls. They already knew exactly who I was. I saw her sitting with some scumbag in a booth. She was in the dress ... again! The same as the first time she wore it. Her face was frozen in panic; he turned, saw me, got up quick and moved to the wall too. I drilled holes in her head with my eyes, pointed to her without a word and made a quick hitchhiking motion with my thumb toward my truck. Without a word, head down, tail between her hot legs, she silently obeyed. At the same time, my peripheral vision saw one asshole about ten feet to my right put his hand on the hunting belt knife he always wore. Without looking, I raised my arm, pointed at him and calmly said "If you wanna know what that tastes like ... take it out .... shit head!" He took his hand off; slowly put it back down at his side. I went to the door, then turned and said "Don't let her come into this fuckin sewer again! If I find her here again, you're gonna pay the fuckin price! ... All of you!!!"

I brought her back to the school without saying a word. Then I did a spanking re-run, but I pretty much tripled it; and this time I introduced her beautiful bare butt to my thick, one foot wooden ruler for the last twenty or so. I heard a lot of "I'm sorry, I won't do it again". That's when I also realized she was high, from the slurring of her words. The bumps on the ride back to my house seemed "very" uncomfortable for her... Go figga?

A couple of weeks later, I was driving home alone, after class, at about eleven at night; no moon; very dark. Larry had already gone back to the house with Leslie so we could run and then train in the three foot lake shallows in the morning, like we did a couple-a times a week. About a mile and a half from my home there was a big Z in the dirt road; very sharp. There were two ninety degree plus angles, about a hundred yards' apart, through a large cattle farm. I had to slow down to about ten mph. As I was just starting to come out of the last corner, on my right, I see a big flash from the dark woods, with my peripheral vision; at the same time a hard thwack hit's the steel frame on the passenger side of my windshield. I knew it was a gunshot, probably a large caliber rifle, the way my whole cab shook when it hit. I was too vulnerable here so I down shifted and floored it, zig-zaging down the road, as to be harder to hit. Next morning we looked at the chunk the bullet had taken out of the truck. Larry and I lined it up; one half a second more and it would have been a perfect head shot. I've always had a real knack for "near misses", like a number of them down in C.A. Hmmmm. Very interesting. Maybe if the assholes didn't smoke so much damn weed they could shoot better. From then on I traveled everywhere armed to the teeth (back then ... I still had some); twelve gauge High Standard riot shotgun with 00 buckshot, my 9mm Browning Hi-Power auto, "Martino," with triple thirteen round mag's in my shoulder holster and a .25 caliber Beretta pocket automatic backup. Oh yeah, a Stiletto boot knife that I could put in someone's head, fifteen feet away. So there, you big ne'er-do-wells; better get me next time! Not that I think a bullet could even penetrate my thick scull. My Pop always said nothing could! I told Leslie to keep clear of those shit heads, but if she heard anything from anyone to let me know ... quietly.

The next day I had my friend, Chick, from the BCI, in his private class. When it was over I told him what had happen. He told me they already knew the slime down at the Cripple Creek were smuggling and distributing all kinds of drugs into the area, since they moved up from NYC and bought the place. They'd been trying to catch them in the act and build a rock solid case against them for a long time. Chick and I were always straight with each other, even though he always knew I was an outlaw; just a different kind from those guys and him. That's when he told me I'd better watch my ass (So ... I bought a small hand mirror for that) because Canada One was their supplier. I'd never heard of them before. He said if they knew I was interfering with their business, they'd be gunning for me, literally. It'd happen to others in the past but they could never prove it. I said I'm not really interfering with they're business ... ehy! Chick asked "You hangin round wit Canadians again?" I'm just trying to take care of Leslie. The Canadian bikers were they're job, but if they ever wanted another gun, I'd be more than happy to tag along! Chick was one of the only two people up there that knew about my other side line; he laughed and said "Thanks for the offer sensei. I'll call you if we need you". Then he surprised me when he added, if I got into a situation and had to take any of them out, don't worry, they'd cover for me. That felt real good! Chick was a good friend; straight up, but a bit of an outlaw himself; got me my legal pistol carry permit in only eight days. Ya know ... dat don't neva happen, man!

One week later, at the same bend in the road, but before the curve, same damn thing again! This time they didn't even hit the damn truck. I gunned it! Fish tailed the Bronco around the corner, killed the lights; two more shots, no hits. I went down the road about a hundred yards out of sight pulled the emergency break an skid to a stop; no break lights! I grabbed the riot gun and ran quietly back to the area hoping to get in a shot ... or ten. When I got close I went to the ground, looked, listened and waited, moving in every two minutes or so. Nothing! Finally, I was almost at the exact spot where they fired at me. Nothing! I waited for something to move. All of a sudden, about two hundred fifty yards or so away (maybe two hundred fifty three yards, seven and a half inches); down past the first bend, I saw head lights come on. A FWD vehicle must have been hidden in the brush. It went flying onto the road and took off like a bat outta hell (but, what da hell would a wooden bat be doin in hell anyway? Wit all dat fira?). My Bronco was too far in the wrong direction and only had a small straight six. That thing sounded like a big V8. There's no chance of catching him; way out of range for my shotgun or pistol. I'd rather he didn't even know I doubled back after him. Maybe next time ... Hawkeye.

A quiet week went by, for a change. No mission calls from Canada; Leslie seemed to calm down a bit. Larry was watching her, so I went down to Dutchess County to visit family for a day. I bought my fourteen year old nephew back up with me to save his life. He accidentally shot his brothers hand from only inches away with a BB gun. The BB was still in him. Just a few days before, the news said a local woman, who was accidentally shot with a .22, was rushed to the hospital, and that the bullet was in her yet. Now ... I thought I was familiar with every part of a woman's body. However, I have no clue exactly where the yet is ... but I bet it hurt! It was late summer; my sister-in-law said "get him outta here before his father gets home and kills'um". So I didn't get to see my big brother, but at least I kept him from killing his kid; for another week anyway! He was a good looking 14 year old kid, dumb, usually stoned ... but good looking. He always liked hanging out with "UNC"; so he couldn't be all bad ... mostly, but not all. At least he had ... good taste. When we got back, Larry had gone to Malone, to his part time job at his father's fried, dead bird take out facility. Next morning, I went into Malone alone; taught a class and came home. Leslie and Brian, my nephew, were "Home Alone". Not quite like the movie! Later, he told me he was no longer a virgin! Leslie had given him his first ... how can I put this ... without being too ... gauche? Uhhhh ... Blow Job!!! Yeah, that's it!!! They were both under age, but at least she couldn't get pregnant; as hard as dat is ta swallow. Brian didn't complain. He hadda start someplace; not complaining! There was certainly none of that! I didn't leave them alone together again; <u>that</u> he complained about! A few days later, Leslie left the school again and didn't come back. We went through the same bullshit again, searching everywhere. I went down to the Cripple Creek again; they all backed to the walls again, but this time I didn't drive my Bronco to the door. The owner said she wasn't there and hadn't been since that day. I believed him; he was shaking an stuttering. I thought he was gonna wet his pants. Days went by, I was going crazy. Larry and Brian were still at the house with me when I got a collect, long distance call. Guess whodafuck it was ... Leslie! Howdahell are ya? Ya little bitch! Stupid went for a ride ... on a motor cycle ... with a bunch of scummy bikers ... to a motor cycle rally ... in neighboring Vermont! They past her around then left her there alone because she wouldn't go back to that place up north with them. Ya know ... Canada! She went to Vermont with Canada One!! She was asking if I would get her home. I was really getting sick of this shit. Now I know why tigers sometimes eat their young (well, you can play with that one yourself. In fact you can go play with yoursel ... never mind)! I sent her the cash Western Union and got her shipped back to Malone. It was a weekend. I went into town, picked her up; bought her home. I didn't want to hear any stupid excuses. Larry said send her home! She's not worth the trouble. This time I pretty much agreed. Brian was still smiling from the BJ a week before, so his opinion didn't count (He probably just wanted to have a word with her... alone). Oh yeah, she was wearing the dress again but at least this time she had panties on; butt not for long! As soon as we got home I took her into her room, put her over my lap again; bared her beautiful rump and started pounding away all my frustrations etc. etc. etc. Brian and Larry were watching the whole time; Brian ... still smiling. Then I asked Larry to get an old flat nylon hairbrush that was my Grandma's. I loved my Grandma but she wasn't actually there. She died on Valentine day, about fifteen seconds after she talked to me, when I was only seven. I have that effect on people. I just had her brush. Maybe this will do the trick? Not the same kind I'm sure she'd been doing the past few days. I laid it on heavy. I've spanked a lot of women and girls, but never like that. The kicking, squirming, crying, begging and I'll be goods weren't working on me this time. She could've been killed and dumped. And ... of all the filth to go with! The guys that were probably trying ta kill me! WTF wuz zataboot ... ehy?! (dat's Canadian talk) Larry and Brian were wincing now with every spank. I think they thought I was gonna spank her ta death. When I finally let her back off my lap she was on her knees, panties an pantyhose still down, looking up at me; tears streaming down her pretty face, rubbing her bare, red, burning butt with both hands and this time it really was a "Hot Ass" in more ways than one. This little bitch was driving me nuts! She begged me not to throw her out. I wasn't even considering that, butt, for her sake, it was best she didn't know that. I cared way too much about her and had grown to love dat dumb little girl. The next morning, she's in the bathroom, door open, standing on top of the sink cabinet, in nothing butt her panties and bra; panties pulled down ... again; looking at her ass cheeks in the mirror saying "Look everybody ... my ass is all black and blue!"(She just couldn't seem to get over her shyness!), with a big smile on her face. WTF! I said if you don't get off that damn cabinet little girl, it's gonna get bright red again! Then she threw her arms around my neck and gave me a big long kiss ... on the lips again!! Damn it; I don't know exactly where those lips have been! But I got a pretty good idea! I love da girl, but I'm glad I heard her brushing and gargling this morning, before she checked out her sore ass. She said "Thank you for caring so much about me. I'm sorry I'm such a pain in the ass." Now, still holding her tightly in my arms, I said "Don't you mean you're sorry you have such a pain in the ass?" She said no, she knew she deserved it. I thought ... maybe we're finally getting somewhere. I was happier than a clam in pig shit! (Even though, back then, I hadn't even invented that particular phrase yet).

Next day I bought Brian home ... so my brother could kill'um. Unfortunately, to the dismay of everyone, he didn't! Even though Brian thought he was on his way to his doom, he was still smiling for the whole five hour drive. Leslie was much better behaved after that episode. In fact, it was the last time I ever hadda spank her. I was glad, I really didn't like hurting her or making her cry; she had enough pain in her life already. However, the biker episode sparked a new problem, connected, yet separate (Remember the yet? I hope so, cause I'm not goin true dat witchu again). Now pay attention ... Goddamn it! It's gonna get nasty!

About two weeks later, Jason, one of my ex-Navy Seal students ... who ate way too fast, said he stopped at a local bar and heard some guys behind him talking about Leslie. He got up to go to the male pee-pee porcelain facility and saw their Canada One, black leather jackets. There were six of them sitting at a table. They were saying how they wanted to find her in town again. He sat back there a while and did a recon for me; just listening, never saying a word to or acknowledging them. Anyway, I told her what we heard and I kept her out of town for a while more. A number of things started happening after that.

Jason, picked up a little more info in the same bar about Leslie, me and a local dealer and smuggler named Birdshit (That's close to his real name, and it suits him, so we'll call him that, cause he's probably outta prison by now). I'd never seen Birdshit (well... maybe on the Malone sidewalks) so I didn't really know what he looked like. No matter; he knew me. He was friends with the bikers; his Canadian suppliers and they all had sticks up their asses for me; like ... Carol Ann.

I really didn't want them; they're smelly, disgusting an unsanitary! But I'm sure that it was very uncomfortable for them, especially riding on bumpy roads! So they can keep their damn twigs! Birdshit, hung out at the Cripple Creek, where he sold his junk ... Wait ... let me rephrase that to prevent a gross misunderstanding; an I mean really fuckin gross! Birdshit was a regular patron of the Cripple Creek bar, where he peddled his drugs. OK? ... The bikers wanted to hook up with Leslie again; Birdshit was pissed at me because his beautiful platinum blond, younger sister, Jackie, who hated him and drugs, told him she was "spending a lot of private, quality time" with me; if ya know what I sayin; his now, arch enemy. Jason said he heard him asking the bikers if they would bring him a sawed off shotgun on their next trip. He'd been asking around town, but hadn't been able to get one. He heard the morons discussing this, and that he'd get rid of me if they'd get him one. Stupid people get even stupider after even one drink, and they're even worse when they're pot heads. Anyway, Jason came up and told me, so I'd be ready for him. I sat Leslie down (the spanking had worn off by now and she could) and discussed it with her. I told her things were getting way too pileated around here (That's hairy ... for you dumb guys). We called her dad and all agreed that she and he should get back together and work things out. To my surprise, she agreed. I put her on an Adirondack Trail Ways bus to Corning, NY and kissed her good bye (which was stupid, since he lived in Albany). At least now I didn't have to worry about her. Oh yeah; I took that damn dress away first!

Not knowing what to expect next, I told Larry to stay in town until I got things cleared up. Driving home on a semi moon lit night, about a week later; about five hundred yards from my, very hard to see, hidden driveway. I saw two silhouettes moving on the road in front of me. They were about fifty yards away and darted into the woods as I came over a little rise in the road. There were no vehicles in sight that I could see. I hit the brakes hard, killed the lights, threw the Bronco into reverse and backed up fast, back over the rise; then jumped out. I grabbed the shotgun and moved in to get a closer look. At least they still didn't seem to know exactly where my house was. Most people didn't. It was so far off the road and even the zig-zag super steep driveway was over two hundred yards long through dense woods. I was on higher ground so I watched for movement and listened. Getting tired of this, I tried to draw them out by standing up and walking in a broken pattern down the edge of the road. I mean, they couldn't even hit me in the damn truck the last two times! Was it the bikers? Was it Birdshit? Was it someone else I pissed off, over some girl? What da hell am I askin you for?? You probably weren't even born yet! Anyfuckinway, I'm moving down the road, ready to dive for more cover, when from the other side, about fifty yards out, come two bursts of fire. I dove into the woods along the opposite side of the road, behind a tree. I don't know who taught them to shoot, but I hope they didn't pay him. Bullets were thwacking the trees above and around me. I started firing the shotgun towards the muzzle flashes but they were a few yards apart and smart enough to keep moving. I changed position a few times too, to make it harder to get a bead on me (I hate wearing beads anyways; it's way too effeminate). I used up the ten OO rounds I had; slung my shotgun on my back and took out "Martino". I guess he was more than they expected to deal with. I opened up, rapid fire, sent them fourteen 9mm rounds split between them; at the same time moving in. I don't think they even had a chance to reload. They never fired another shot. I sent a fresh thirteen rounds their way, then reloaded again and waited, crouched to the ground. I waited about a quarter hour; nothing moved. I couldn't pursue safely because clouds had now covered the moon and it would've been stupid at night anyway. I don't know where da hell they went and I wasn't staying around to find out. I back tracked up the road to Bronc; turned around, lights off and went back to the school for the night. I didn't wanna give away the location of my home, in case they were back in the forest watching. I never heard or saw a vehicle anywhere that time. Next afternoon, I came back to the spot where they were (fully re-loaded+) and found a lot of empty .30-.30 shells. It was early fall now and the wet leaves were all disturbed and pushed up into the woods for a long way where they ran in their hasty retreat. Don't know who, or why for sure; or how they got out. Maybe they spent the night pissing their pants in the woods. Nothing like that ever happened by my home again. I guess they thought it'd be a lot easier than it really was.

The next week I had a four day mission to Guatemala. When I got back, Jason came in and said he heard that Birdshit had been drinking and bragging to his friends how he was gonna blast me for screwing with him, as soon as he got his gun (Butt? ... I could've sworn dat was his sister!!! No wonder he's so pissed off). I never even met, or knew what that idiot looked like, except for what his sister Jacky and Jason described to me. I didn't want to endanger the students, so I canceled classes for a week but kept going to the school. On my desk, in a long slender cardboard box, my end open, the front closed; fully loaded with 00 buckshot an facing the door, was my shotgun. "Martino" was stuffed in my karate gi, full of hollow points. I made sure people saw me come in, in the morning; go upstairs into my office, whose door faced the entrance door. I had a folding bed, shower, fridge, hot plate and plenty of food, coffee and tea. I was being kind-a like human bait. I even left the door unlocked and put a big welcome sign on it ... And on the third day I arose ... (Oh no wait; that was some other guy ... with a beard ... I think). On the fourth day Chick F. stopped in for his private class. I forgot to cancel his. He saw what I had and said "Forget it; last night, we finally gottum!" On a tip, they caught them at a drop point in the woods with a huge load of weed, coke and pills; bails of weed! It was being delivered by Canada One. Chick said "Birdshit was there! He won't be going anywhere for a long, long time ... years! Oh yeah, there was a sawed off shotgun (a federal offense on top of everything else!) and ammo in with the load! I guess that was for you, Sensei; ha, ha, ha, ha."(<Chick) ... "HA, HA, HA, HA" (<Me). (I only laugh in CAPITALS; it's a strict policy of mine).

Anyway! No one else ever tried to shoot me; ... well ... not in Malone anyway. I heard from Leslie about nine years later. I was living in a condo downstate, with two other beautiful "Hot" teenage girls ... butt legal this time, 18; that I also hadda bare-ass spank ... a lot! Vicky yelled "A girl named Leslie's on the phone; wants ta talk ta you". Leslie tracked me down; I don't know how. She just got married; and of course, she was already pregnant! She was with her mother in Tucson, Arizona. She thanked me for the spankings again; "for blistering her butt", as she put it. Her mother got on and did the same. Her Mom said it must have changed her life; now she was doing great. That made me very, very happy. I always wondered how she made out when she went back home. I'd only heard from her one other time a few months after she left. Like I said, with a stubborn, misbehaving female, a good spanking always works! Just like Eddie told me it would. Stellaaaaaaaaaaaaaaaaaaaa! (On The Waterfront; Marlin Brando ... <u>and Eddie</u>!) *******

My good friend / student / back up, Larry, like most of my old friends, is gone now. He's probably hanging out with my big brother and my friends Constantine, Billy T., Frankie, Will, Seiko Shihan Oyama and Chipper. I hope I see them all again ... soon. I really miss him too.

*A true fuckin story by: Tony Fuckin Z (Except, I lied about my Teddy Bear........his real name was..... Yahnush)

And so ... a new adventure begins ...

The Secret Lives of Tony Fuckin Z *or* <u>*El Guerrero Que Venga Los Nino's*</u>

In early 1972, I was operating my Kyokuninjakan Martial Arts Dojo, on Main Street in beautiful downtown Malone, New York. The school already had a reputation for being very tough with no bull shit, hard defensive, street and military type martial arts. That's why we didn't teach kids (that's where the money is). I was soon to find out it even spread across the border into nearby Canada, only eight miles away. One day two young men, Marty and Rich, obviously in exceptionally good shape, walked in between classes and said they'd heard about the place. We talked a bit and they asked if they could stay to observe a class. I said sure, so they did. That was the beginning of another great adventure. They said they've visited many schools and styles and never saw classes that intense and long anywhere, so they joined the school immediately. They were very good eager students but I could see something more and different in them. As if they had a purpose. A few weeks went by till one day they stayed back after class and asked if they could talk to me privately. That's when I found out they were mercenaries working for a multi-millionaire Canadian plantation owner, with plantations in five Central American countries. He made his money in coffee and bananas (personally I prefer cash; too much coffee makes ya nuts and the bananas rot in a week). The short story is they wanted to recruit me. They had no idea I was already trained by ex-Special Forces, anti-Castro Cuban guerillas and was a U.S. Air Commando, but they said they could see something intense about my teaching. I said, "Take me to your leader. If I like him and the job, I'm in!" But absolutely no one else can know; there's already enough rumors going around about me here.

When I was introduced to "Claude", I liked him immediately. He looked about 65 or 70, and stood about 5'8", with white hair, soft spoken. He told me he needed some good men to protect the people, "families", who worked on his plantations and made him rich. He was a good and caring man (Odd for a multi-millionaire). Claude paid his workers four to five times as much as anyone else did. He covered all their medicals, housed them free and even had chapels, schools and supplied teachers for their children on the plantations. He even let them grow their own food gardens and raise chickens and livestock for food, if they desired. He didn't allow children under 13 to work at all. He even continued paying his elderly workers, who could no longer work, one half of their old salary with all their other benefits. The people loved him. He had a beautifully, unselfish, caring heart. I already started to love him! Especially when he said the job paid $1,000 a day ... cash! From when we got on the plane till we got back off. All expenses, medicals, shots and such included. Even ammo! He even was thoughtful enough to take all our personal information to notify our families and other loved ones in case we were killed as well as the ranking students from my school. The missions were short, basically to handle any trouble that came up, especially anyone who tried to harm "his people", as he put it, in any way. He didn't care who the hell it was, in or out of uniform. The governments didn't care. They didn't want to lose their piece of the action over a few greedy little, would be dictators for fear he would shut down his operation in their country. The problem with these two bit shit-hole countries is the corrupt governments don't really give a rat's ass (but who'da hell would want one anyway?) The governments didn't care about the people as long as they're making money. They assign slimy little "dictators" to an area, and give them Carte Blanche. Usually, this is La Policia' (The Police; not with Sting, they weren't even around yet) the words that terrorize the people more than any others. The ones that are supposed to help and protect the people are their worst nightmare. They steal, rape, torture even kill and they're armed to their rotten teeth. When Claude explained the situation to me, I would've gone for nothing! But I didn't tell him that. I took the Goddamn job! But first I had to get my equipment ready. No, not that you disgusting pervert; my guns and stuff! <u>That's</u> always ready! Then get a thousand or so shots. I felt like I took a hit from a damn mini-gun; and most importantly, get a cat sitter. Ruby Ann Begonia, then the love of my life, had to be looked after by someone I trusted, who really cared about her. Sarah, who I sometimes dated, worked at the Veterinary clinic where Gonia was spayed. She loved Gonia and Gonia loved her; Perfect! Sarah, Gonia's ... gynecologist, didn't know what I was doing but I said if I didn't show back up someday, my precious Gonia, would allow Sarah to live with her. She was a little bit suspicious (Sarah ... not Gonia; I briefed Gonia on the situation before I left. I knew she wouldn't talk) but happy with that. So I went back to my above board life for about 3 weeks or so itching for the action I hoped would come soon. Then finally the call came. I told the students I'd call them all when I got back from working down state. Then I called Sarah and hugged and kissed Gonia ... a lot! We usually got a day or so notice before embarkation. My first mission was to Guatemala. Not a big deal to break in on. Slap some sense into some slimy Policia, "town cop" types; (I really enjoyed that!) give a strong warning, and like that ... we're gone. They only had a small force of about eight or nine that we could see. They didn't seem inclined to be interested in having any trouble from us; Not for now anyway. Not that it really mattered much, where ever the hell we went. We eventually went to four of the five countries while I was there; they all looked and seemed the same to me; incredibly hot humid jungles. Even when they were mountainous they were miserably HOT and HUMID! I HATE FUCKIN HOT and HUMID!!! I love cool and cold; even snow! Lots of bugs too! BIG ones! I got to see giant spiders, biting ants, mosquitoes, Labrador retrievers, poisonous snakes and 6" long poison centipedes. I HATE FUCKIN CENTIPEDES! ... Even

more than hot and humid!!! And I ain't crazy about them Goddamn dogs either! O.K. no more whining; at least it was non-boring action. That made up for a lot. Not to mention a "G" a day in all American CASH! The best part was we got to help people doing it. My childhood dream had finally come true; I'm a hired "Gunfighter". Silly, but I grew up in the late fifties, watching way too many westerns. Like most kids my age, my other dreams were to open either a combination Custard stand/Chiropodist office, so people could have their feet worked on <u>while</u> enjoying really great ice cream; open a religious bakery called "Amazing Glaze" Or be a professional Manure Salesman.
****

… "They owe it to us" …

We got a new guy in about a year and a half after I started, when I was leading the squad. He was a bit of a "brownnoser" with me. Like Marty and Rich who brought me in, Al was another ex-Canadian paratrooper. He seemed semi-ok but unlike the rest of us, very self-serving. Nothing too odd, but he didn't quite fit in. Claude asked us to give him a try. He went on three missions with us; all were to a Nicaraguan coffee plantation. He did his job but the crew told me he seemed to have an "un-healthy" attachment to very young girls around eleven or twelve. There were a few of them there, and he was always talking about the ones he saw in odd ways, so the crew was keeping an eye on him. We worked very hard to win and keep the trust of these fine people, for their sake, as well as Claude's. They considered la policia' their worst enemies and any soldiers with guns frighten them. Even though they knew we were there for them and all worked for the same boss; they were still leery of us. Our mission to Nicaragua was the same as most, either warning someone or making them pay for not heeding such. We were there for five days this trip. Oddly enough it wasn't la policia' this time. A small gang of eleven bandits were terrorizing the area and it took us a while to catch up to'um and adjust their bad attitudes. Not that they needed them anymore. Every once in a while, somebody has to flush; it keeps the stink down. Anyway, the manager's wife had invited us to come in, while she was kind enough to make us some great local food. As usual, we had given all our rations to the children in the nearby village. Al, the new guy said he was going out for a pee. He was gone a looonng time for a piss. The woman was still cooking when her young daughter came in, head down, and went directly to her mother. Their backs were to us, but we could see she was sobbing. We'd brought her a box of candy this trip for her birthday. She just turned twelve the week before. Claude even kept track of all the children's birthdays. Her mother put her arm around her and held her close. Then we saw that she was sobbing too. It seemed as though they were trying to hide it. They were whispering in Spanish and the mother was trying to comfort her daughter. Marty was our interpreter, so we went up to them and asked what was wrong and how could we help? She told us that the soldier with the bird tattoo on his arm raped her in the shed. Al was the only one of us with a tattoo. He had an eagle on his left forearm. I guess it meant he was tougher than us. I went outside and there was Al, calmly smoking a fuckin cigarette as though nothing happened. Why not? No one just scarred him for life. He was also the only one of us that smoked. First he tried to kill us with his second hand chain smoking on the flight down; now this. Now I had two reasons ta kill'um! I walked over to him and I could see that damn smart ass look on his face he always got, when he knew someone was about ta say something he didn't like. I confronted him about what he did to the little girl. His response was "They owe it to us". I guess a thousand plus a day just wasn't enough for someone of his obvious worth. By now, everyone was standing outside. I growled, "We're here to protect these good people; not pray on'um, asshole!" I reminded him of how hard and long the rest of us worked to win the trust of these good people, not to mention how he scarred this sweet little girl for life. On top of that, I had warned him about his very obvious "unhealthy" attraction to very young girls (children) on two other separate occasions, while on other missions to this very location. The second time I told him if he ever forcefully touched any woman, especially a child, I'd shoot his fuckin dick and nuts off. That was before I learned the lesson, you never warn anyone twice. The second time, they always assume you're all talk. I asked if he remembered what I said the last time. He turned away and very smugly answered, "Yeah, right! ... Like that's gonna fuckin happen." At that point I pulled out "Martino" (my Browning Hi-Power, 9mm auto); the first round was always a hollow point. I was still eating my tortilla thing the mother had made me. Yeah! Yeah! I know; I should'na been talkin wit my moutful; Tuff! ... Blow me! Den yours'll be full too! ... He was standing five feet away, right in front of the shed where the slimy piece-a filth raped the little angel. I pointed Martino at his groin and "cocked" it (amazingly ... no pun intended). He said "Hey! Dat ain't funny! Alright! Alright!! Alright!!! I'll never do it again!" I said "Yeah ... I know!" Then I did exactly what I warned him I would. It took him about a half hour to bleed out. During that time the father, hearing the gunshot, returned from the fields. When they told him what Al had done to his sweet little angel he went over to his wreathing body and kicked him square in the face. Then the mother and daughter spat on him and called him "Puerco" (pig)... I kept eating my tortilla; it was really tasty. We each apologized to the young girl and her parents for what happened. Unfortunately, there was no way to undo what happened. The little girl wrapped her arms around my chest and gave me a very long hug. I tried to hide the tears rolling down my face in her hair, kissing her beautiful little head, as I hugged her back saying, "I'm sorry", over and over. We all apologized to her and her parents for the terrible thing that happened to their precious baby. Later, I tried to apologize to my men, but they said no; if I hadn't done it, they would've. Later the workers disposed of his body in the jungle. He didn't deserve a burial. They said he acted like an animal, so let the jungle have him. Then Marty said "We don't hurt kids; we just hurt people who do". He repeated it in Spanish, to the people too. That said it for all of us. We never took anyone else in again while I was there.

My squad was a great bunch, brave, dedicated, super tough, deadly and very caring. Except for that one piece of shit, they were some of the best and absolutely, most trustworthy men I was ever privileged to know. They risked their lives for those people, me and each other many times. I would've died for any of them and I have no doubt they for me. Their word meant something; I trusted them! I can't say that about most of the people I have known in my life. They weren't there for the money; they just got paid for doing it. It's not the same thing. Claude understood why I had to do what I did, and why I had to do it, in front of the people who trusted us; and him. They came first and now they really knew it ... Besides, Claude didn't like smokers either! Oh yeah, I bought him back some of the great tortillas too ... he loved'um!

I'm enraged many times when I hear stupid, know nothing, imbecilic, usually gutless people who do nothing for anyone but themselves. Running their stupid mouths about "mercenaries or merc's", like they know what da hell they're talking about. Talking about them as though all mercenaries were evil butchers that will do anything for money! Mercenaries are just private, paid soldiers, that pick their own battles and causes, instead of having slimy, crooked governments pick them for their usual, under handed, self-serving, economic purposes (ya know, like the U.S. and the oil companies in the Middle East, Viet Nam etc. etc. etc.) It's usually the most misinformed people that are the most opinionated. I was a sergeant in the Air Force for over 7 years. Our government military gets paid too. As always, there are good guys and bad guys. But if a mercenary loses a leg, arm, eye or anything else, there's no long term or any medical help or veteran's hospitals for them. Or any other benefits that normal soldiers are eligible for. They're on their own! That's one reason why they need to get paid so much. And if they're killed, their bodies usually stay where they fall. No going home or expensive family funerals. In a different country, for a different cause, a couple of years later, 12 of us went in on a mission to help a group of people. Due to a bad recon, 3 days later only 3 of us came out; 1 wounded. The rest stayed where they fell. We barely got out alive, quietly jumping a freighter out of the country. It was a bad day and a bad job ... And I lost Freddy!

Most missions were similar to each other in nature. Not the shoot one of my men's dick and balls off part; the dealing with la policia' or bandits stuff. Except for the three with Al, there were never more than six of us on a mission, after "Crazy Dave" left. Dave was a great and caring guy. He was older but had really bad Malaria. Not that there's any good Malaria. We really missed him; he was a really good leader. We did have one excellent, but part time member of the regular team; Jock (Well, he was Canadian, what da hell else did you think his name would be ... ehy?) another ex-Canadian paratrooper, but he was also an executive body guard who couldn't always leave on a one day's notice. That's why we were trying out Al. We were always outnumbered and out gunned, but I've always had a thing for that scenario. Even in street fights, I like to use their numbers and the consequent over confidence and confusion, on their part, against them. It's what I teach in my Kyokuninjakan schools. Marty asked me once if we should get more men. I said "No, cause that'll just give'um more targets ta hit". He said "While in one way that was very logical, it was also "Fuckin Nuts!" I said "You gotta be fuckin nuts to do this kind of work anyway. Besides, Steve McQueen, Yule Brenner, James Coburn and Charles Bronson already did it with seven. We do it with only six!!!" *******

... The Horror ...

The worst mission we ever had involved la policia' in El Salvador (the proud home of MS-13). One of Claude's biggest coffee plantations was having real, consistent problems with them. It haunts me to this day and for some reason much more now that I'm older; maybe because now, I have a precious little granddaughter. I have nightmares about it two or more times a week; get up, pace the floor and drink a lot of brandy trying to sleep. Sometimes I'm not able to go back to sleep for fear of having another episode. Occasionally, the nightmares wake me up in tears. Sometimes when I'm driving the memory comes to me or I see something involving children on TV and I have to leave the room as the water works begin. I hide it from my wife. She doesn't really know much about my past ... or care. This mission changed my life and my personality. I always loved children, even when I grew up, when the other adults sat together and talked. I always went and sat or played with the kids. The kids loved it and so did I. They love it when an adult pays enough attention to them to play with them. They're so beautiful and innocent, until we adults fuck them up. After this mission though, I became paranoid about all children's safety; but most especially little girls.

It was about five weeks since our last trip when we got the call. El Salvador, the worst shithole of them all! And the worst experience of my entire life. La policia' there were especially rotten. We had run-ins with them on a few occasions. (I'm already tearing up just thinking about it. Some hired gun!). The chief was a real piece of shit. He and some of his main boys had a bad habit of getting drunk, going out to the farm, roughing up and robbing the workers; sometimes even raping the women. They had heavy numbers and were heavily armed; the few unarmed workers were always helpless. The plantation managers in all the five countries Claude owned, had direct communication with him, and, as I found out later, with each other. Claude was sending us down to give them "another" warning. I had already given them a couple of strong ones, and again, only about five weeks before on our last trip to that rotten hell hole. That time the chief told me they didn't like outsiders interfering in "their" business (in Spanish; Marty translated). I told him the plantation was not "their" business. It was ours. I didn't want to keep warning them, because I know every time you do that after the first, they believe more and more you're bluffing. I don't fuckin bluff! That, enhanced by the fact that there was almost twenty of them and only six of us gave him a bigger than normal pair of "dumb" nuts! The biggest and only reason I have nightmares is because of what I did before the mission.

That week I had promised one of the girls I was dating in Malone, that we'd spend an evening together at my place. She said I was neglecting her and we hadn't been together in over a week. I promised her we would that weekend. She didn't know what I did. No one did! To her I was just a martial arts instructor. Claude's male secretary called on Thursday saying we needed to go Friday. I already promised her we'd have Friday night; no matter what! I don't break promises! I knew Claude only wanted me to go down and give them another strong warning. That's what the secretary said. But I already gave them three, there's no way they'd think anything different would happen. Claude wanted to avoid violence whenever we could. We understood that because it could get complicated. I, however, wanted to go in and wipe out that filthy fuckin rats nest. Marty and the crew all agreed. They'd already gone way too far; way too often! Especially, with the rapes! As squad leader, it was my call. I decided to wait another day and leave on Saturday, instead of Friday. I didn't want to break my word and we were just going down there to give another stupid warning anyway. However, the horror we found when we got there was the worst thing that ever happened in my life; before or since. As our chopper landed, some of the people, along with the really badly beaten manager, came over to us with painful looks on their faces; like I'd never seen before. Marty started speaking Spanish a mile a minute and they back to him ... all at once. I didn't know what da hell they said yet. But I knew it wasn't good. Then Marty turned to me with a rage in his eyes I had never seen before; tears running down his face. He started telling us what they said. My gut churned and I clenched my teeth; now tears rolled down my face and it spread instantly to all of us. I said "Those aren't men; they're fuckin monsters and this call's for "butchery"! Killin's too damn good an too fuckin quick for'um. They need to be in Hell <u>here first</u>; before we send'um there!" Eight of la policia', including the chief, had come to the main house the day before; drunk! They ransacked the manager's home an took everything. Then, not believing they had it all, beat him senseless. Three of them, gang raped his wife. But that was only the beginning. They kept the helpless workers at bay with their AK's; tied the two parents to posts and made them watch ... screaming and struggling, as they gang raped and sodomized they're two screaming, terrorized little girls. All eight of them! The two little sisters were only nine and seven!!! Both little angels died from the shock, trauma and injuries ... One day sooner. It was <u>my Goddamn fault</u>! We would've been there when they came. If that, so called, "Wonderful" God himself came down and got between me and them, I'd of shot his fuckin balls off too! None of us spoke another word. We wiped our eyes, loaded up, got in a truck and took off for the village. The manager wanted a gun too. We never took any workers with us before, but I completely understood. I gave him Martino, and all my mag's.

When we entered the village everyone but Roger, driving, jumped off both sides as we approached their barracks. He drove the truck right into the front of the building, taking out the whole wall. Then we all came running thru the hole he made in full auto fire. There were five of them inside, but they never got a shot off that I saw. One was under the front driver's wheel; still alive; one leg on each side. He was screaming; it was on his groin an nuts! Perfect! I couldn't ask for more. Then all hell broke loose. There were a bunch of those slimy shitheads out back; we wasted no time, but I wanted the "eight" alive if possible. We all did! I kept the father close to me, to ID the monsters that destroyed the little angels ... and their lives. The shootout went on for at least five to six minutes, maybe ten; it's hard to tell time in a situation like that. Eventually, they started raising their hands. Something I didn't expect. Then I realized one by one, they just ran out of ammo. We caught them with their pants "still" down.

The surprise and ferocity of the attack had really caught them off guard. They weren't all there, at the beginning. Some came running from the village hearing the gunfire. Unfortunately, for them, they ran into Roger and Matt. All in all, there were eighteen of them. When it was over we'd killed ten. Three more were gravely wounded. Two were "gut shot" an unfortunately, only took about a half hour to die; screaming and begging us to either help or shoot them (yeah ...... maybe later). But at least they were in the agony they deserved. The other had his shoulder partially blown off and unfortunately, bled out in only a few minutes. The important thing was "the eight", did we get them alive? Maybe there is somebody out there watching. The father pointed to one of the gut shot guys as one of them; not the rest. They got off easy; they just died. The five pieces of shit that surrendered, however, were all there, including the chief. I guess they were his main "Bros"! The ones we wanted the most!! I've been prone to a killing rage many times in my life, but never like that. I could see the hell in the eyes of the father and my crew. We vowed no one in this village or plantation would ever forget this damned day.

There was no sound now except the agonizing moans of those three wounded ...... things. Listening to them was like a beautiful song bird to my ears. I felt absolutely no remorse or mercy towards them; then or now. If I could have kept them in that state, they'd still be alive now, over 43 years later; begging to die, waiting for the gates of hell to let them in! All I could imagine was the terrified screaming of those two little angels and their horrified parents. I told the men to tie their hands tightly behind them. Now they were kneeling, begging for mercy. Yeah!! Right!!! Even the chief who spoke some broken English, but no one answered them. Not even the father; we all just stared coldly. There were some long drying racks for something in the rear of the building. It didn't matter for what. Whatever they were used for before, they had a new, more important purpose now. We stripped their clothes completely off and hung them naked by their feet on two of them; upside down, legs spread, facing each other, about six feet apart. Then I told the men to back off. If there were any repercussions for what I knew I had to do, I didn't want it to reflect on them or Claude. I'm in command, I take full responsibility. I had the crew rip gags from their discarded shirts. Then I used one rag to hold their dicks as I slowly sliced them off ... one by one, shoved them in each other's mouths; then gagged them so they couldn't spit them out. I wanted them to feel what the little girls felt when the monsters did it to them. They fought bleeding, gagging and trying to breath. The father just stood there, with a blank sad stare in his eyes, tears running down his face. Even after over 43 years I can't even begin to think about any of it without crying; like now, thinking about those two beautiful little angels. They used to bring us all flowers, whenever we arrived. They didn't even understand what was happening; screaming for their helpless parents to help them. In a silent daze, we all watched the filthy monsters wreath in terrified, agonizing pain (like the two little Angels); trying to scream with their full, gagged mouths for more than a half hour ...... until I thought about the children again. I said "It's not enough!"... I took my Gerber fighting knife out and sliced their rotten bodies open from groin to throat; gutting them like the filthy animals that they were. Then Marty carved, "Dijora los ninos solo", on their writhing backs. It's Spanish for "Leave the children alone". Unfortunately, it only took about another few minutes for them all to bleed out and die. We left them hanging there. Roger backed the truck out of the building. We took all their weapons, ammo and anything else the people could hide and use and went home. When we returned, we had the burial for the two little Angels. I've tried, but I've never been able to write about that. On our own, we extended our stay five more days this time, in case there was any more trouble; free of charge to Claude. I took no pay this mission.

Two days later, this stupid, twenty-something, sanctimonious, Bible bullshit preaching, Mormon, missionary bitch showed up at the plantation. I guess the villagers told her what happened. Like we gave a flyin shit! She started preaching her religious bullshit to us, "me", about the terrible thing I had done. Never mentioning a word about what those monsters did to those little angels or expressed her outrage or even condolences to the grieving parents. I told the insensitive little bitch, we kept them from hurting all the others they would have, if we didn't stop them. I had all I could do to keep from bitch slapping her ta death. That little know-it-all, know nothing, bible spouting ass hole said "It's up to God to judge them". Swallowing my killing rage I replied "Too fuckin bad he couldn't bother to show up and help those poor little Angels! And besides ya stupid little cunt, I didn't judge'em; I just moved up their court dates! Now get the fuckin hell outta here before I pull those pants down and spank your bare, dumb, worthless little ass raw, little "Moron" missionary! ...... Leviticus: 69:69". Then the crew laughed their asses off again ... It was the first time anyone even smiled since we got there. I couldn't; they didn't know it was my fault. Or... let me know if they did. And so again, later, as always, we re-attached their asses for future use. After that, I <u>NEVER</u> WARNED ANYONE <u>TWICE</u> or put anything or anyone before a mission. When somebody needs killin ... just fuckin kill'em! ...... before they hurt anyone else. Don't talk and wait! When we got back, I informed Claude about the "multiple warning" policy bullshit. In the immortal words of Tuco, from the Good, the Bad and the Ugly; "When you have to shoot ... shoot! ... Don't talk!" And if he wanted to get someone else, for da job, he should go ahead. He wasn't ecstatic about the way I did it; ya know, the hangin, de-dickin and guttin thing. But he understood why, and the men all backed me, without exception. The same as they did with that other piece of shit "Al". They told him they'd quit if I went. It was the children; they got to all of us ... him too. People die or get killed every day; a bullet's too damn quick and painless. Only, so called, "civilized" people think killings enough; even worse ... too much! These deserved much more and much, much worse.

La policia' were so hated by all the people in all those countries; we found later the government who-evers, were told the rebels did it. O.K., that'll work! I really didn't give a flyin shit, but we didn't want to complicate things for Claude. He was too good a man and doing too much good for those poor people, for us to screw it up.

A few weeks later, we landed on a coffee plantation airstrip back in Nicaragua (no, we didn't go back there ta visit Al's dick). It was the strangest thing the way the people looked at and greeted us. We had been there many times before. They were the same people but now something was very different. The women and many of the children greeted us with flowers and local food at the landing strip. We were bringing food for them and candy for the kids (so they could have rotten teeth too, ya know ... like American kids). They were smiling and talking in Spanish, low among themselves. OK, but why the hell are they watching me? And mumbling? Did I forget to zip my fly??? Again!!! I was feeling real uncomfortable. I asked Marty what the hell they were doing. What's going on? What da fuck are they mumbling aboot ... ehy? Marty said, "They gave you a title. You are now ... El Guerrero Que Venga Los Ninos'". I said, "Whatdahell does dat mean ... ehy?" He smiled and said, "You are now: The warrior that avenges the children". That's when I found out Claude's plantation managers, in no matter what country or what they produce, keep in touch with each other, as well as him. Something I didn't know before. They share info like one big family. They apparently shared the stories of the two incidents, in house, with all the others. After that, it happened in whichever country we worked. The women and children always greeted us and brought us flowers. It always would tear me up like a damn wuss; … and the other guys too; it wasn't just me! And they always referred to me in that way. But we all did it; not just me … A lot of it had to do with Al. I guess because he was one of our own crew. Now they all knew <u>they</u> really came first. I just wish it wasn't so "after the fact" and could've been "protects the children instead of avenges". The damage had already been done, and the children were already hurt … or dead. We still had to deal with, fight and kill the filthy policia', and bandit groups on many occasions; in other places but we never had another serious incident involving kids again, while I was there.

The nightmares I suffer are always much the same; we get there too late …… because of me. The little girls suffered, horribly and died, because I put myself first! Something I'll never forgive myself for. I've never had any regrets at all about what I did to those filthy monsters; except that I didn't do worse and make their agony longer; just in case there really is no fuckin hell. And mostly that I blew off my responsibility, when I should have been there for those kids. I should still be there disposing of more pieces of shit like la policia' and the Al's of the world. That's where I belong. Not here with these stupid "so called" civilized, people that haven't a damn clue what the real world is like; the absolute merciless brutality that's out there. TV can't really show them. Besides, they're too busy guzzling beer an "watching da fuckin game". Somehow I stepped off my path. I shouldn't be here. I hate it here. Again, every once in a while somebody's gotta flush! That's what I did best. Here, I'm just another fuckin asshole loser. I just keep seeing the children, just out of my reach, screaming for help, like they did with their parents; but like them, I'm always helpless and too damn late! I can't even watch a TV show where children are hurt without crying. I hope writing this down, getting it out will help the nightmares go way or at least lessen their frequency; even though I know I deserve them. An old school friend I ran into years ago, who became a therapist once told me this might help, if I couldn't or wouldn't talk to anyone; I should write about it, like a story or a novel. He didn't know what it was about. I said I couldn't tell him. I need brandy every night just to be able to sleep at all. I wish it was all over, so I could cash in and get down to the other hell and out of this one. I don't really want to be here ... or anywhere, anymore, but my little Angelic Granddaughter, seven now, still needs me to be here, for her, a little longer. *******

... A Scorpion and a Snake? Holy Shit!! ... I Want My Mommy!!!

We got the call for a mission to Guatemala, on a fall Sunday evening. It was about three weeks since our last mission. That one was to Honduras, where Keenan broke his left ankle, when he stepped into a hole in the jungle, while running for cover. We were taking fire in a jungle clearing from another rebel band (They weren't very good; they didn't even know how to play "Stranded in da jungle". I guess they were just too damn young,). They'd been plaguing the banana plantation, on an off, for several weeks; mostly on. Anyway, we spent nearly a week there, but again, we were unsuccessful in catching up with them. After they fired on us and we returned fire for a few minutes, they melted back into the dense jungle they knew so well. We needed to take care of "The Keene One". It was a really bad fracture, and he was in a lot of pain. His foot was crooked and badly swollen; instantly. Claude recalled us, saying another time, another day. We were pissed; it was our third attempt with that slippery bunch.

That coffee plantation in Guatemala where we were going was the largest Claude had; a few square miles in size. Again, like in Honduras, it was easy for them to raise havoc (instead of coffee. I guess havoc is easier ta raise) and melt back into the jungle without ever leaving the plantation itself. It was like, looking for a machine gunner in a hay stack ...... or something. Besides, even though they weren't working on the plantation, they were probably living right on it, in the jungle; rent free!! They were much more difficult to track down than la policia'. We always knew exactly where to find those shitheads ...... from the stink! This pack of shitheads was different from most of the other bandit groups we encountered, with the exception of the ones we kept "almost" catching up to in Honduras (in the paragraphs above this one. This is for the people who didn't understand "pileated" in the Canada one story ...... again)! They were every bit as adept in the jungle; their jungle, same as the Hondurans in theirs (This is even getting confusing to me. I'm forgetting which country I'm writing aboot ...... ehy). We were good, but we were visitors; no match for them in some ways, on their home turf. They were like the jungle trees themselves; but a bit more dangerous. They had automatic weapons. The trees just had leaves and bugs (like I said; a machine gunner ... blah, blah, blah). It would take a lot ta nail both'a deese groups. This would be the longest mission we ever had; almost a miserable week and a half; lotta cash; lotta misery. The temperature was always well over a hundred degrees in the day and dropped to a "frosty" ninety eight or nine at night, with about ninety percent humidity. "Whatdahell am I doin here?" kept racing through my head. I love winter and snow! This mission, we had to take on a guide or we would never find our way through that Goddamn jungle. Of course ... his name was Juan ... what else? He was a little shit; one of the plantation workers, about 25 years old. The manager said he grew up in that area and knew that jungle like his own back yard (his back yard must'a hadda hell of a lotta Goddamn snakes). We were also fortunate, though, in that he spoke some broken English. We armed him with one of the AK's we took from another group of bandits on a previous mission there. They didn't need them anymore. We started searching for the group in their last known location, where they had assaulted a group of the workers at one of the remote areas of the plantation. It was so large that there were smaller camps, like small villages and several were spread throughout the plantation, with rutty dirt roads an trails connecting them. As usual the bandits would rob the workers of everything they had; even food. It was the price the workers paid for being treated so well by Claude. We all felt bad about it, but that didn't mean we could allow it to happen.

Juan was a better than decent tracker. He picked up their trail as soon as we arrived at the area, when the village people ... (No ... not those guys; no dancing, no singing, no silly costumes. It was just too damn HOT fadat shit!) showed him their last exit point. Tracking them through that jungle for four days was absolutely miserable. We slept on net hammocks at night, to keep from being eaten alive on the ground by centipedes, ants, spiders, mosquitoes and scorpions ... Oh my! We encountered more snakes there, than on any other mission I was ever on. That was especially true the fifth day when we finally encountered the bandits, by a deep muddy stream we'd just waded through (where I lost my favorite Stiletto boot knife). All of a sudden two bursts of gunfire came at us. The squad all scrambled and dropped for cover. It was hard to tell exactly where it came from in that heavy cover, so we all laid on the muddy banks waiting for more. Marty and Matt both gave some return fire, as the rest of us waited to try and locate the source and exact direction of the attack. There was no immediate response, so we laid there for about five minutes, waiting for something to move or happen. That's when I looked over and noticed that Rich, who was about twelve feet ... seven and a half inches (maybe eight) away from me, had a scorpion climbing up the back of his leg. I whispered to him, pointing to my leg, trying to alert him of the danger. He looked down, saw it, and was about to swat it off, when in a louder whisper, I said "Freeze!" My eye spotted the large head of a Fer-de-Lance just emerging from the brush between us, no more than four feet from Riche's head. (All snakes are deaf and almost blind. They only see blurs and react to movement and body heat and have absolutely no access to modern hearing aids). The Fer-de-Lance is responsible for more snake bite deaths, than any other snake in the Americas. It's big, very aggressive, and extremely well camouflaged, with nearly two inch fangs. Rich saw it and froze; (even in that damn heat!) fuck dat scorpion! He's small potatoes! ... Well ... The snake had to know he was there, because he's a pit viper (the snake ... not Rich). He had to pick up Riche's body heat when his forked tongue came out, especially at those temperatures. Then it moved completely out of the brush, into the open and started to coil about three feet from Rich; all seven feet of him. He had a large, heart shaped head (again ... the snake ... not Rich. Rich had a regular head; ugly .... but regular. Yeah ... that's it; his head was regularly Butt Ugly!) Marty had hit the dirt only about six feet to my left. Rich was on my right. By now, he too was aware of the situation. If Rich got bit, it would be extremely difficult, if not impossible, to get him out of that dense jungle, to help. Even a chopper couldn't find us in there. Not with that thick canopy, so it would've done us no good anyway ... even if we had one! Marty crawled quietly toward me using my body to cover his movements (I told him he could ... just this once). It was one of the tensest moments I'd ever experienced on that job, and there were certainly no shortage of those. The damn snake seemed to be enjoying terrorizing Rich; it moved around a little, then finally settled and coiled, about two feet from his leg; looking straight at him the whole time. Possibly, it might have been trying to determine whether Rich was a threat. If he knew Rich personally, he'd of known he was a good guy. Well ... except for the killing stuff... I mean; otherwise he was harmless and obviously too damn big to eat. The scorpion was still just sitting on his calf. It almost seemed to be watching the damn snake, like we all were. I thought it might be a Mexican Stand Off between them two, but ...... we were in Guatemala! All of a sudden another burst of fire came from the jungle in front of us; it had the staccato sound of an AK-47. Nobody moved! They apparently didn't understand how busy we were. The snake didn't know about the shots; he's deaf! Marty took his silenced Mark 2, Ruger pistol from his pack; then slid a few feet up the bank, on his belly, by my head, to use it for a rest (my head ... not the bank). He needed the increased angle so he wouldn't hit Riche's leg, since Rich was frozen in place. I couldn't believe he was gonna take da shot (I was really hopin he wasn't tryin fada scorpion). The snake was so damn close to Riche's leg. He rested the butt of the gun on the side of my head, right on my ear, while I watched Rich; then he fired; it was just that beautiful "thphew" sound I love; just not on my damn face! The bullet hit the snake and took it a couple of feet further down the bank with it. At the instant he fired, Rich pulled his leg up and with a quick swat, swept the scorpion off. He was obviously pre-occupied observing the whole damn drama (the scorpion …… not Rich). Marty made a great shot; caught the Lance right in the scull. Rich smiled … gave Marty a little "thank ya" salute ……. ya know; then rolled over and took one of the longest pisses I've ever witnessed (must'a been at least an hour …… maybe an hour an a half). We just laid there twiddling our thumbs. Then we hacked off his head, to save him for dinner later (again … the snake … not Rich … he'd a been too damn tough anyway). The rebels must have either pulled out, or temporarily just lost interest.

Roger and Jock both fired short bursts in their general direction, but there was no response. Or maybe there was a Fer-de-Lance or Bushmaster over there too. OK! Nuff fuckin aroun; back tada job! After Riche's two hour piss (that damn situation would've scared all da piss outta me too), we packed up and continued carefully through the dense jungle, trying to re-acquire contact with the rebels. A few hours later, near dusk, we entered a small jungle village. Juan then realized we'd wandered off the boarders of the vast plantation. From the looks on their faces, the villagers seemed very frightened of us at first; at least till Juan and Marty both started talking to them, in Spanish of course, explaining that we weren't there to harm them, in any way. They told them we were just chasing a group of local bandits. Then an old man, who looked about a two hundred, dat seemed to be the head or "Elder" of the village, began telling Marty and Juan that those same bandits had been praying on them as well; for a long time. Now, it seemed ta make them real happy to see us. I don't know what the hell they could've been taking from them; they had nothing. The poor children were begging us for food; once they realized we weren't there ta harm them. As we walked through the village the kids came out of the woodwork, grabbing onto our legs, begging for food. We gave them all our field rations; everything we had. Unfortunately, it wasn't enough. There were so many of them. Marty said that's what the old guy said. The bandits had been coming in and taking whatever food they had. I've never really understood why they didn't just live off the jungle; we did and we weren't even from there. They knew that jungle a lot better than us. There's so much small game an birds on the land, fish in the water and fruits in the jungle (lots of free, fresh coffee too). Anyway, when we all were done with our pathetic crying over the hungry kids hanging on our legs, we vowed to get rid of those scum balls at all costs; even if we had to stay for free! Juan told the Elder so, and that he should tell his people what we said. Besides it would make good relations for Claude too. We even cooked up the Fer-de-Lance for them over a fire pit they had in the center of the village. We were real hungry that night, but not as hungry as those poor people. This village wasn't really our job ... or business, but those poor people and especially those children had to be helped, and there was no one else tadoda job. And besides, we hadda get ridda those filthy slime balls for Claude and "our" people anyway. Then it hit us; they're all "our people" ... even if they're not on the plantation; except for the slime balls of the world ..... all of'um!

That night, we slept in our net hammocks again, at the edge of that small village. Next morning we set out to try and pick up the trail of those shit headed bandits. We all agreed that our general consensus was; if we kill them all, they will no longer need to eat ... therefore, they will no longer have a need to take food from the kids! How damn simple can it get? They were also robbing money and food from Claude's hard working plantation people; throwing in an occasional rape. Soooo ... we backtracked to the general area by the stream where we had encountered them the day before, when they sent that damn snake and his partner the scorpion to distract us till they got away. We really didn't even know how many there were (not snakes and scorpions; we already knew there were just the two). However, the old man at the village said sometimes only three or four bandits would show up; other times as many as eight. We seriously planned on cutting those numbers down even more; to aboot ... zero ... ehy. Especially since they were even taking the food out of the kid's mouths; ... dats a niet, niet (dat's Russian talk for... a No, No ... are ya Impressed wit my use of foreign languages?)

Juan finally picked up their trail by some supper good luck, not to mention amazing skill on his part; then the damn show off found a bunch of AK shells on the ground, about a hundred fifty feet from the muddy stream bank, where they pinned us down the day before. I was getting ready ta bitch slap dis kid; he was makin us look like amateurs ... or was dat ... us? But I'm sure glad he was there ... We all were. Finding the exact spot from which they fired at us, in that dense jungle was almost a miracle to begin with. Even actually finding our way back to the exact spot where we were with the snake, was amazing, and it was all Juan (we were no longer actually with the snake; the people in the village ate him). Not to mention finding the AK shells! (Yeah, yeah, I know ... I already mentioned it ... Blow Me! I'm tellin da story; ya don't like it, go buy some'a Vonnegut's whinny bullshit! ... Mine's real!) Roger said maybe we should ask Claude to put this kid on the payroll, if he wanted to be; whenever we're in town. We all agreed; at least in Guatemala. He was really a great kid too. No kiddin, we felt privileged and damn lucky to have'um there. But we just worried about gettin'um killed; that wasn't his job.

Juan picked up their trail through the bush from their last firing location. He followed them like a blood hound through the jungle for four more days (occasionally, lifting his leg ta pee on a tree and mark his territory). Bees, bugs snakes; bees, bugs, snakes! It wasn't like they were careful (the bandits ... not the bees, bugs and snakes); once he had the trail it wasn't that difficult to follow. They weren't very careful covering it once they moved away from us. Maybe they thought their crawling, slithering compadres and a few shots would scare us off. Oh contraire mon frère! It'll take a little more den dat ta scare us off! Not much ... just a little.

On the fifth day since our last contact with them, when we were just coming up from wading across another two foot deep jungle stream, another hail of gun fire came down on us from a hillside we were moving towards. There were a lotta shots hitting the water and trees on the opposite bank; about fifteen feet away ... maybe ... almost sixteen feet ... four and a half inches. Fortunately, it seemed no one ever taught them how to shoot downhill! You always have to aim lower than the target. It was a lot of gunfire; seemingly coming from at least half a dozen or more weapons and locations on that ridge. We flattened out on the bank ...... again; waiting for another snake to show up. These guys have a thing for streams! Now they had to know for sure we were after them. We started returning fire; but not too much. We carried a lot of ammo; me most of all, for "Freddy", but you can still waist it and run out! I hadn't seen a single Mercenaries-R-Us supply store since we got there! Anyway, we returned fire and decided since those two legged rectums, that were so good in the jungle, couldn't shoot downhill, we should use that fault and start moving in. Especially since they probably couldn't see where their bullets were landing. They were shooting way over our heads. So we formed a fairly tight line, only about ten feet apart; maybe ten feet, eight inches or so, and began moving through the brush, towards the hill they were on. We didn't want to lose them again. Matt stayed put but moving occasionally, in heavy cover, darting behind trees; returning fire. The idea was to make them think we were all still down there. We moved as carefully as we could trying not to disturb any more foliage than we had to. For all we knew, they might think we were still back at the stream; and we wanted to keep it that way. Roger said he had a snake of some type in front of him at one point but he quickly hacked it with his machete. We wanted to keep our line moving at the same distances and speed to keep track of each other. We still didn't know exactly how many there were. As we reached the edge of the bush close to the base of the ridge we stopped, under cover, using hand singles to communicate. It was still a real dangerous location since they were above us on the high ground. They were still firing ... at Matt; nowhere near us now; way over our heads. We decided to try and flank them by moving toward one side and up the ridge, past the last gunner we knew about. They were only about a hundred-fifty feet up the hill. Maybe a hundred and fifty three .... feet ... four inches (we were too busy for a precise measurement). Soon we were actually above them and moving into positions over those clowns (it must'a been so hard ta walk through the jungle with those big stupid shoes; an damn hot wit all dat makeup) pinpointing as many as we could. They were still shooting down at Matt when we opened up dispatching the immediate ones that we could see first. <u>We knew</u> howda shoot downhill! That immediately drew fire from the others, exposing them to us.

That was great except for one thing. Another one popped up in back of us, further up the hill, from out of nowhere ... well ... da jungle. Matt had opened up from his position behind a tree below again. Now both they and we were in a cross fire. Fortunately, we already got most of them. All of a sudden, Jock yelled "Rich's down!" Shit! Half of us fired downhill and half at that sneaky prick above us. He went down in a hail of extremely fast moving, portable holes. When we checked later, he looked like a human colander! It only took a few more minutes to eliminate the others; there were eight in all. It was, however, one of the longest shoot outs we ever had. I was sorry "The Keene One" missed it. He always had a thing for chaotic gun fights ... ya know! Fortunately, Rich was only wounded. The real crazy part is he took a bullet clean through his left calf muscle. Right where that Goddamn scorpion was sitting!!! We poured a small bottle of peroxide on the wounds and covered them with two sanitary napkins to limit the bleeding and keep them from getting infected till we got the hell out of that miserable jungle. We had to carry him across the streams, filled with germ and parasite infected water. Now all we hadda do was spend more than another day walking home, in a b-line by our compass and Juan, through that damn steaming jungle. Obviously, we were carrying Rich most of the time. We were gonna leave'um but ... he was a student of mine. Heat, humidity, bees, bugs, snakes! When we got back, we all voted to give Juan $1,000 each. He earned it! Down there, he'd be like a millionaire! And Claude paid him even more when we told him how great the kid was.

Oh yeah; ... next trip to Guatemala, only a few weeks later, to deal with la policia; we bought a bunch of cases of non-perishable foods to that off-plantation village; as many as we could get on Claude's plane. Beans, rice, vacuum packed meals etc. We paid Juan to get us back there; he knew a "short cut" and we used a pick-up truck from the plantation, this time ... cause we sure as hell weren't gonna walk! It was the first time we saw those people since we left them, chasing the bandits. They seemed a lot happier to see us this time. The kids brought tears to our eyes again, but at least this time, they were happy ones. ....
Dumb Wusses! *******

... A Little Song ... A Little Dance ...

The Honduran mission, one of my l last, was like most; a show of force and warnings to leave the plantation people alone. The problem was the local assholes causing the problems didn't like "gringos" telling them what to do (it gave me flashbacks of El Salvador). Only three weeks later we were back there in a shoot-out with the same slime balls after they visited the plantation, badly beat the hell out of half a dozen workers, then robbed them of their money as well as the food in their homes. The manager said it was a fairly large force of about fifteen men or so. He was among the victims. There were only six of us; our normal operating force. Claude had us flown in on his private aircraft to a remote jungle airstrip. No customs, no passports, no nuttin! I doubt if we'd have got in anyway with the weapons we were carrying! In some places we landed directly on the plantation; in others to remote airstrips where there was a chopper or truck waiting to take us the rest of the way. When we got in we were met by the manager of the banana plantation who briefed us on the situation. We split up into two trucks and went to the small village about five miles away, where la policia' HQ was. Parking the vehicles in the jungle just outside the village, we wanted to arrive unnoticed ... on our terms. This town had a substantial force and we already knew they were well armed; mainly AK's, some older sub machineguns and pistols. Unfortunately, one of them spotted us entering the outer edge of the village. They must've been expecting trouble because without a word, not even a, "Hey! Suuppp dudes?" He opened up with a burst from his AK-47... or 48 ... I don't know; they all sound da same ta me. Not very hospitable at all! We spread out and within seconds there were half a dozen more laying down heavy fire on us from two small buildings. A minute later, the number doubled, then more! It was as if every filthy cop in Honduras was after us, so the only thing we could do was start building up our "kill ratio". That rood bastard that wouldn't say "Hi", was the first one down. It wasn't me! I'm glad nobody told those idiots, it's not a good idea to shoot at guys carrying automatic weapons, from windows, in houses with paper thin wooden walls. I raked the sides of both buildings with my best friend "Freddy"; my .30 caliber, IBM, M-2 Carbine. Freddy was like E.F. Hutton. When Freddy talked ... EVERY-BODY LISTENED!!! Marty, an ex- Canadian paratrooper was a few yards to my left with his AK and doing a hell of a job. I think he shot the "rood" guy. Anyway we were fortunate not to lose anyone but there was way too many for us to handle in this situation so we had to pull back and re-group. Sometimes that Goddamn jungle can be your best friend. Centipedes and all! We laid down a lot of fire and kept the ones that were left down while we made a hasty exit. About half way back to the trucks, at a bend in the road, we melted into the dense jungle (that'll give you an idea just how hot it was!), laid down in a half circle pattern and covered ourselves with foliage in an ambush we knew they'd walk right into in their haste to get us. That's when I think the rest of the team began to think there was something wrong with me ... again! There was only about six feet between us; I started giggling. Uncontrollably! The men were on both sides of me, heads down to the ground, looking at me like I was insane ... (like?). I covered my mouth, burying my face in the bug infested dirt in an effort to stop. But that just made it worse! By now la policia' were only a few yards away. It only made me giggle harder, tears in my eyes! Now la policia' were almost on top of us. I thought one of my own crew was gonna knife me just to keep me quiet! We could hear them whispering to each other in Spanish. I don't know why but all that kept going through my fuckin head was "A little song, a little dance ... a little seltzer, down ya pants"; from the old Mary Tyler Moore show, "Whatdafuck wus zataboot ...... ehy? Well ...... ya know ... I was working with Canadians. An instant later we opened up and cut'um all down; first from the ground cover then jumping up screaming as loud as we could to shock and confuse them. It worked! They were no more than twenty feet away and barely fired ... wildly! Nine more hit the ground. All theirs! Our only casualty, a bullet went thru the front of my camo air commando hat, thru my hair and out the top back, as I stood up. Our ears were all ringing from the gunfire. Six assault rifles emptying a half dozen thirty round mag's on full auto, plus theirs, add in all the yelling and one asshole, still laughing and yelling, "MARY! MARY!! MARY!!!" at the top of his lungs, makes a hell of a racket. Afterwards, Marty asked me if I was nuts. Still laughing I said, "Ya gotta yell. I can't hear ya; I got seltzer in my ears!" The whole crew laughed their asses off when I explained. Then we picked up all the weapons, ammo and money we could find and gave it all back to people they stole it from. We told them to hide the weapons and ammo. Later, we re-attached the crew's asses for future use. Another mission completed; amazingly, no casualties; ... cept my hat! Most of the missions were similar, though only a few were as intense. I participated in twenty three from early 1972 to late 1975. Only two students upstate knew of my triple life as a full time karate sensei, lecherous womanizing pig and part time mercenary. I eventually became the squad leader, around 1973, sometime, when "Crazy Dave", the leader, who also had Malaria, decided it was time for him to retire from the life. I served in Honduras, Guatemala, Nicaragua and El Salvador. I never made it to Costa Rica. Claude didn't seem to have many problems there. I doubt if I missed much. It was probably just another hot hell hole like the others. Though the rest of the crew said it had the worst jungles. I became somewhat attached to the people in all of those miserable places; more especially the children. It broke our hearts, all of us, to see the poverty and misery they had to live with. Not on the plantations where Claude took great care of his people. He really cared about them and treated them like his own children and with great respect, but in the villages where the children would beg us for food. It's not often you see grown men, mercenaries, gunfighters, crying like babies, but so many times we did. All of us had great respect for Claude and we took great care to earn his, as well as the trust of those good people. But Claude couldn't support the whole country that's why all of us started spending most of our pay bringing food and meds back for the people in the outer villages, on our return trips; sometimes even small toys for the kids. It was just selfish on our part, because it made "us" feel good to help them, and we didn't cry like little babies .... as much. *******

You'll pay me How Much?!?!?... What's a Fort Worth?!?!? ... Anyway?!?!?

In 1989 I was running my martial arts dojo and FFL licensed gun shop, fairly successfully. My biggest and best friend (and I mean that in many ways, he was well over five hundred pounds; mostly heart) Big Ray, and I, got together to do a bit of body guard work; among other things. Something we had both done before, individually; but never as a team. Ray was a walking tank. He, like me, did a lot of bouncer work too, in some pretty nasty places. We figured between his size and power and my martial arts, as well as other experiences, we'd make a good team. We had no idea where this would lead, but we were both adventurous outlaws, so we gave it a try. At that time "Big Bear", as people sometimes called him, was also a sports bookie. This gave him a lot of connections (mine were only electrical) to certain underworld "personnel"; including many particular individuals of "Italian descent"... again ... like me (I'm Sicilian; <u>real</u> Italian)).

One of our first assignments was a bit to the side of normal body guard work. It was more of a favor for a well-connected, ridiculously rich guy, and close partner with the bookie end of our Italian brethren. He, along with his close friend and business partner, the then, President of Mexico (they grew over one hundred acres of marijuana in Mexico, for sale in the U.S.; it was guarded by the Mexican army), supplied huge sums of quick cash (as well as weed) whenever it was necessary. It seems a local twenty year old drug dealer had taken his young, adorable, but dumb, fourteen year old daughter on a date, she obviously was not supposed to be on (kind of reminded me of Leslie back in Malone NY, in the Canada One story). But as we all know, young girls are usually attracted to the wilder ones, until they find out why they shouldn't be. Anyway, this twenty five cent, feces consuming, mammalian fornicator, slapped her around when he brought her home; then date raped the poor girl in her own driveway. Of course he didn't know what her father was. He, her father, made most of his "above board" millions in the airline insurance business. I guess he thought her old man was just a wealthy insurance salesman. Ray and I saw the pamphlets on the plane ride down with his name, his company and his quarter mile long office building. You got a million dollars in airline life insurance, for one flight, for just a buck. Anyway, he couldn't use any of his own "people" in Fort Worth because the punk lived in Dallas; right next door but in a different county. The sheriff in his own county worked with / for him, but the Dallas sheriff was after him, knew his people and wanted him bad, so he steered clear of Dallas, county. They needed people from "outside" to come in and inflict the "penalties" the punk had earned defiling his little girl (and who knows how many more). He didn't want the piece of slime killed; just busted up so bad he'd never do anything like that again. The guy who got us involved, was the second biggest sports book in NYC at that time (and yes ... that means ... those Italian guys ... again). Sometimes we collected money for him from rich guys, who liked to collect when they won, but didn't see why they had to pay when they lost.

He also knew me and how I felt about people hurting kids; especially girls. They all, kind of, left it up to me just how we would deal with him. He said "However you please; just don't kill him." As much as we wanted to, and knew he deserved it, we had no intention of doing that. And we made sure they understood that. I'm not a "hit man", but I'm certainly more than qualified for da job. I did guarantee he would never do, or "be able" to do, anything like that again; to any woman; young or old!!!

Ya know, I'm writing this story from memory but it just occurred to me that unlike in all my others, I haven't fuckin cursed once! Oh ... well, that should hold ya fa now. I'm sure there'll be plenty more, later along with some stupid puns; ya know? Be patient, Goddamn it! It's hard for me to think funny when I'm writing about anyone hurting kids or women; and his sweet young daughter, whom we met, was both. I would like to have done an "Al" to him, but I can't do that here ... as easily. (Reference to Episode 2; The Secret Lives of TFZ).

So we land at Dallas, Fort Worth airport; then get off the plane (We find it's safer to do it in that particular order) and a tall, real friendly, African-American driver picks us up in a white limo; so much for staying low key. He was a great guy with a cool sense of humor and we all got along fine. He was even told to buy us all our meals, which I'm sure our employer paid for. Anyway, he was to take us wherever we needed to go, since he really knew his way around his home turf. They put us up in a luxury sweet, at the local Holiday Inn; all expenses paid, as was the flights down and back; with fuckin room service too!!! (See; told ya there'd be more profanity; if you were patient). We started tracking this poopy-head down as soon as we got settled in. First we checked all of his known hangouts. We were given the info but didn't know where it came from. We searched day and night for two days; nothing. No one knew where da hell he was. We even went to his house; where he lived with … his mommy. No one was home. My intension was to break both his knees and elbows, then kick his nuts hard enough to pop them both; and yes … I can dodat! (I wanted to make him "a broke dick dog"… like in "Predator"). I hate rapists! And I hate child molesters! And, I hate child molesting rapists MOST of ALL!!! This punk will wish we'd killed him when we're through with him! On the third day we called his mother on the phone. I said we were friends of his visiting from out of town and couldn't find him anywhere. She said he just went to prison. He got convicted and sentenced to 3 years for something he'd done many months ago. How'bout dat … ehy? Now the little punk knows how that poor little girl felt. He's over 18, its Texas, so they'll put him in with the big guys; not the teens. That's almost better than what I was gonna do. Maybe when he gets out, we'll get called back to finish the job I was <u>sooooo</u> looking forward to. We reported it to our temporary employer; he was happier den a clam in pig shit; about the prison sentence I mean; not being in pig shit; only clams like dat. Dat's why they're always smiling.

That night, our driver picked us up in the limo and took us to a beautiful country club, with an eighteen hole golf course (The only thing more boring than golf, is reading about someone else's adventures. Ya know … like you're doing right now), to have dinner with his boss before we flew home (my arms really get tired, but the flight is a lot tougher on Big Ray because of his weight. His arms get so tired and he gets winded easily, so we have to land and rest every couple-a miles). It was great. A secluded private table, great food, some good booze; then, we found out he owned the damn place! The whole damn country club; it was even nicer than "Bush Wood" (ya know, in Caddy shack), but they still had gophers. Unfortunately, in Texas, they were the size of bull dogs! Anyway, he kept trying to hire me as his personal bodyguard. Big Ray, as usual, kept making me out to be Superman. I kept trying to tell him, I was more like Lois Lane; ... my girlfriend at that time. He offered me crazy money, but I didn't want da job. Finally, I said "OK, I'll meet you half way ... I'll take da money ... but not da job" ... He said "No!" He told me he'd give me and Lois, our own house, two cars, totally new, clean identities, free club membership, all medical and car insurances, all travel expenses, no utility bills plus $75,000 a year... in cash; with bonuses of ten to twenty five thousand each, for any "special jobs" as he put it. I said "No, I'm worth at least double that" (I was just kidding, so he'd back off. I knew what he really wanted was his own private hit man) without blinking an eye he said "OK, you got it". I almost fell off ma damn chair. WTF! I stuttered a second, then said I'd go home; talk to my girlfriend, Lois, and think about it. That wasn't easy to turn down! Ray looked at me like I was nuts, but Ray didn't understand what he was asking for; I did! After that great dinner, we went out to the parking lot, to his new BMW, where he opened his trunk (the one on the BMW; he's not an elephant). I thought Ray was gonna have a fuckin heart attack! It was full of cash! And I mean <u>FULL</u>! I've never seen that much money, before or since. It literally filled his trunk, front to back; side to side, top to bottom. I won't leave twenty bucks in my car! Its' gonna be a real bitch if he gets a flat and needs to get at that spare! On top of the pile was a Bersa .380, automatic pistol he wanted to show me and ask my opinion of, since he knew I was an FFL gun dealer back home; and basically, a weapons expert. Then he grabbed a fistful of hundreds (Hey, we're in Texas, he just grabbed "A fistful'a dollars". I wonder if Clint's around.) I think everything in the trunk was hundreds; It was getting dark, he was talking to us; looking at us; didn't look or check for anything specific in there, just grabbed it off the top while he was talking to us, like he already knew exactly what they all were and peeled off thirty each. If even half of that pile were hundreds, there was at least a couple or three million plus in that trunk. Three

G's cash each for three days, plus all expenses paid! ... I was starting to feel like I was back in Canada working for Claude again ... ehy! I said "But we couldn't doda job". He said "It didn't matter; we came when he needed us", that's what mattered to him (obviously, it wasn't a "cash flow" problem). Besides he still had a little task we could help them with on the way home. The limo brought us back to the Holiday Inn, where he later, showed up at our room carrying a large gym bag. When he dumped it on the bed, I thought Ray was gonna have the fuckin heart attack he almost had before in the parking lot; or at least a stroke. About a dozen or more huge bundles of cash, in medium to small bills came out; about ten inches long each. He said it was sixty five pounds of cash we were to deliver to people who would be waiting at the airline terminal in New York. It was $485,000 in cash. He said we should count it. I said it would take a week! We'll take your word. Big Ray just stood there, just staring at it. It didn't really impress me ... it wasn't mine! ...<u>That </u>would've impressed me!! But it did fuckin surprise me (I just through that one in for you profanity lovers; ... ya know?). Anyway, next morning our limo came to bring us to the airport. The temperature was already well over a hundred degrees, by the time we got there. I spent a lot of time in Texas in the service. I always hated the damn place because of the damn heat; 110 / 120+ degrees all the time. I'll be spending enough time in hell when I'm dead. I don't wanna be in hell here too ... although ... I was married ... twice!!! I was carrying the bundle. So, between when I placed it into the X-Ray unit; walked ten feet through the metal detectors, to the other side and saw it come through, I lost about five pounds ... in sweat! And it had nothing to do with the damn temperature! I was trying ta think of great excuses why I was carrying a bag with 485 G's in cash ... Uhhh ... I lost my wallet! ... Uhhh ... I don't like using credit cards! ... Uhhh ... I might wanna buy extra drinks on the plane! ... Uhhh ... I'm a big fuckin tipper!!! So sue me!! .... I'll pay you in cash!!! ... WTF! ... OK! ... No bells, no alarms, no security! Nothing went wrong ... dat alone seemed unbelievable! (Back then there was no metal fiber in the cash).

We had a good flight home. Big Ray had the bag under his seat ... seats; he needs three; damn good thing those arm rests come up or he'd a hadda very long and extremely uncomfortable flight. Now we're here, in New York airport, walking out in the arrival area and there're four big, really ugly fuckin guys; more like gorillas, (come ta think of it ... their knuckles were touching the ground!) standing together; looking real serious (an again ... fuckin ugly ... Yeah ... dat's it ... they were seriously fuckin Ugly). I think at least three of them had bent broken noses. I thought about asking them if any of them were named Moose or Rocko; but ... I refrained (<That's the first time in my whole fuckin life I ever used the word "refrained" (2) in a sentence. I guess I always, refrained, from using it; and that's the third; I'll try to refrain (4) from using it again)! The big bookie, that went down with us seemed to know who they were. At least I hoped ta hell he did, cause without a word, I handed them the duffle bag with almost half a mill in the "Italian peoples" cash! The next day we found out that the guy they were using to do the transporting job for a while, before we just did, picked up the cash then took a different flight to whodda hell knows where? With three quarters of a mill in small bills! I guess he just needed the right amount to risk his life for (been there; done that; but with me it's always been reasons, not money; not that I have anything against money). They'd never stop looking for him! And they won't "just" kill him, if and when they do find him ... Dumb bastard!

A few months before, they found a young guy, in his twenties, a close friend of one of my nephews (the only one dumb and lazy enough to get involved with these guys), in the trunk of a stolen car, in the long term airport parking area. People said a horrible, sickening stench was coming from the car. It was a hot summer; it was his rotting body; he had a baseball bat hammered up his rectum (that's his asshole ... again ... for the guys who didn't understand "pileated" from the Canada One story). That's what killed him! That poor kid was just a runner they "suspected" of pilfering a few bucks, when picking up bets for one of the big bookies. It was obviously to make an example of him; warning others ... Real nice guys!

This little episode, while not very exciting, was to open the door (or gates) to a true, much bigger, even sillier one ... Maybe, even "prison gates" this time! ... Ya know? *******

*** But looking back after 40 years ...... <u>I wish I took da fuckin job!!!</u>
****

Me and Big Bear ...... We're Here Tadoda Job .... After Lunch!

After a few more similar but uneventful assignments, we were approached by an "in the business" associate (that's a classy way of saying he was a crook), and told that a friend of his in Croton, NY, needed a favor from him; which, naturally, meant from us. Earnest was a nice guy; crooked ... but nice. Unfortunately, eventually we would find that he wouldn't live up to his name. He had a successful contracting business in town. He also had another friend in on this caper (Hey, I love capers. Remember, with the curly anchovies. I told you that in the Canada One story); a moronic nitwit restaurant owner named Gino; incredibly stupid and totally untrustworthy. Well ...... this should be interesting. We had our first "consultation" about da job at Gino's restaurant one afternoon, when the place was closed. It seems a friend of theirs was thinking of divorcing his wife (that should be fairly obvious; the wife part, I mean. Who else would he be divorcing? But I put it in anyway, for those people who didn't know what "pileated" meant; again, back in the Canada One story. Try ta keep up ... Please!) Anyway, it seems this piece of extruded fecal material, friend of theirs had a very successful local bar. The IRS, however, never got wind of just how successful it was since "somehow" he "forgot" to tell them that he had been making money, hand over fist and skimming the cash for years. While of course, he was still claiming he was still losing money ... ya know? Are ya wit me so far? He kept this cash in a six hundred pound safe in their home. He hadn't yet informed his wife about his intentions to divorce her, even though she was about to give birth to this turd's, second child. It also must have slipped his mind, to tell her he was shacking up with one of his waitresses; ...... regularly; in their home! When she wasn't there! Hell-of-a guy; he's up for husband of the year! Anyway, he wanted them, to hire us, on his behalf, for $2,500 each, to stage a mock burglary and get the safe out of his house, to a "safe" location. Since he knew his wife knew of the cash, and would go after it and him, in a divorce case; as well as their beautiful home and kids. The key was that even though the safe would be burglarized, it couldn't be reported to law enforcement or insurance companies, since it was skimmed money and she knew it! A Hell-of-a ... "combination". (Sorry, I godda do deese dumb "safe" puns, cause I godda reputation ta live down to). Are ya still wit me? (Don't worry; I'll get some foul language in soon. I just don't wanna make this any more confusing than it already is, for those who didn't understand "pileated", again ... ya know ... from the Canada One story).

OK, we're at Gino's restaurant; they laid out da job and left it up to me to come up with the perfect plan to pull it off. We accepted the deal. Now, Gino says "Good! You guys want lunch?"... "OK ... we could use a nosh" (dat's Jewish talk. Jewish Canadians would say "We could use a nosh ... ehy"). He makes us two giant, hot, breaded veal cutlet subs; on the house. Why he didn't make them in his well equipped kitchen is anybody's guess. I told you he was stupid. That ladder was so damn dangerous! They were really good, loaded with melted mozzarella cheese. Big Ray wants double cheese, cause he's trying ta lose weight ... he's on the well-known, melted mozzarella cheese diet! Knocks it down in four bites, then, also has a giant, double slice of apple pie. And of course ... the mandatory ... giant "<u>Diet</u> Coke"! By now, I'm thru half my sub. Large Raymondo says "make me another one ta go Gino, double da cheese this time, and of course another ... giant "<u>Diet</u> Coke" .... We leave; get in the car, Big Ray opens up the other sub and starts eating ... as I'm getting into the other side. I said "thaaaat's quite the diet you're on old buddy. I'm sure glad you're keeping your promise to me about losing weight, and not drinking that damn regular Coke. I hear that shits murder on your waist line! Now I'm driving Big Ray's SUV ... He lost his license, now he don't drive (ya know... like Joe Walsh said). He starts talking to me about da job, waving his right hand around. He accidentally hits the windshield with the back of his (ham) hand and cracks it. I'm damn glad it was his car. He only moves his right hand around when he talks, cause ... he's only half Italian.

OK, I start the planning. We have to do this in day time, when no one's home; but we can't attract attention from the neighbors ... soooooo ... we need something here. I don't know what his wife did most nights, maybe the same as him ... but ... with a waiter; I didn't ask why, but normally she wasn't home. One night, I wanted to go in solo and make it look like they were being robbed at gun point, but he said no, cause later she might realize it was a set up, so that was out; also, he would've had to open the safe and give me the cash. Besides, I thought about it and I didn't want to upset a pregnant woman with an armed robbery; especially, in the last months of her pregnancy. It could hurt the baby. It'll have to be day time, when no one's there. We needed to set it up with him, to make sure it's on the right day ... at the right time. At that time, Bell Telephone was the areas phone utility. I decided it was a perfect mask for the operation. I needed to do a lot of studying and prep. Exactly, what car they used; color, model, year etc.; also I needed the right signs, uniforms and license plates. A friend of mine owned a sign shop that pressed out magnetic signs and plates. He just finished making hundreds of magnetic signs for, guess who ... Bell Telephone! I said Kev "make me a few more, please". I got license plates, in a large dark parking lot, at night ... like my 57 Caddy hub caps when I was a teenager. You only take the front ones, so you don't screw over the innocent owners. Most people hardly even know they're gone, and don't report them missing. Or they just assume they fell off. Leave the back ones; they're what the damn cops look at. It doesn't matter if they match! Nobody matches front and rear! I got a fluorescent, white tape at a local hardware store to cover and alter a couple of letters anyway. At that time New York plates were fluorescent white with black numbers and letters. I found the perfect car at a rental. The uniform and clip board was no problem either. I did add a gray wig and grew a mustache to look older (and not be so devastatingly handsome), just in case a neighbor tried to describe me later. The rest of the crew dressed like work men … really ugly workmen! This all took place over a number of weeks. While this was all going on, we were still in constant contact with our man in Fort Worth. He still, kept bugging me to move down there to work (kill) for him. I told him, Lois and I hadn't decided yet (No! … Nooo! … Not the yet thing again!). If it was anything but a hit man, I'd have probably gone for it; … well … not a male prostitute … OK … maybe! Butt, I'd only take female clients; ya know … Janes … instead of Johns.

Then we also needed a reasonably new, white pick-up truck or van to haul the safe in … "safely". Rentals have too much printing. We borrowed a white pick-up from a friend for a few bucks and put the signs and plates on. Then we got a blue tarp to cover the safe with. We didn't need the car anymore; it was just for the recons. I wanted it to be seen by the neighbors in the driveway a few times, to establish our presents (not that we'd be bringing any. It wasn't even close to Christmas); looking as if we were working in the area or making system repairs. From here on it'd mostly be the truck, with the signs; or both. That should keep their noses off of us when it was "Go time". So … Anyfuckinway! (<there, are ya; happy now? I don't have ta curse … ya know… I just like it! Cause I'm no fuckin good!!) Now we're just waiting for the perfect day, and time. Meanwhile, back in the jungle, Ray, my excessively proportioned compatriot in non-legal activities, brought in two other guys. He was already acquainted with both. He thought we'd, need help loading it "safely" onto the pick-up (yeah, I'm getting tired of 'um too). One of them I knew; but I wish I didn't! It was my one and, <u>only</u> … <u>no good</u>, nephew. Someone who just can't keep his damn mouth shut. No, not Brian; my brother spared his life but he's still wondering why? However, Brian still has that damn smile on his face … I think its permanent!

In the interim, for some dumb reason, I can't recall why, Gino wanted to have another meeting with Big Ray and me. He said he'd come up to meet us in our area; buy us lunch and we could talk. OK … you buy us lunch … it doesn't matter who you are or what the hell it's about; we're there, dude! Oddly enough, we meet at a local restaurant called Gino's. No relation to the nitwit restaurant owner we're disgracing their fine establishment with. It's mid-day; lunch time; everything was already set, but we believed Gino wanted to <u>play</u> "I'm a Mafia guy" <u>with himself</u>; no reason. There was nothing left to discuss; Butt … he's "buying us lunch" at a nice restaurant, soooooo … pic a table! Gino immediately starts talking gibberish (which I believe, is only spoken in … Gibraltar). He's going on about da job, as though he's gonna do it. We're in the center of a crowded restaurant; he pulls a pistol out of his pocket and says "Tony, what do you think of this?" He's waiving it around, pointing it at Ray, me, and everyone else; it's a loaded Bersa .380 auto, same as our man in Texas had. The difference was he had a working brain! I grab it; cover it; put it down on the table saying "Not in here Gino!" Then he says he doesn't know "If" he should get a permit for it … "Ray! … Next time … we eat at his place … again!"

OK! … Today's the day. No one's home; no one's gonna be home. We got the "Go ahead" from the owner, through Ernie. He said "The coast is clear" … not that dat mattered to us; we're too far inland for that to make a difference anyway. It's a very hot, clear, sunny day; about 1:30 PM. We back into the driveway. Everybody goes to their assigned tasks as quickly and efficiently as possible. Two men go around to the back of the house facing the woods (the house faced the woods … not the men). They break a window to make it look to his wife, like the burglars got in that way. He left his custom built, $2,500 front door unlocked for us. It was two inches thick, solid hardwood, with two special, double keyed dead bolts. So we wouldn't have to destroy it. I'm in the driveway, acting as look-out; writing on my clipboard, like the crew foreman; (Well … I was) ready to deal with any problems with nosey neighbors. Absolutely no one was allowed to bring any weapons, of any kind. If anything went wrong, I was the shield; the buffer, so no one would be injured or killed, on either side, if anything went wrong (except, maybe me). I wore a full, Second Chance bullet proof vest under my shirt. I also carried a, non-lethal, stun gun and a spray can of mace. And then ... there was me! They covered the safe with the blue cloth tarp, Bell's colors, to bring it out (it also nicely brought out the color of my beautiful eyes). When the two of them and I, leaned it on the tailgate; then tried to lift it onto the pick-up bed. We couldn't! The Large Bruin growled "get da hell oudda da way! We'll be here all fuckin day!" He grabbed the safes bottom (whatta perv!) and with one lift nearly through it onto the truck. I knew he was strong, but I had no idea how! I thought the truck springs were gonna break when it came down; the bed dropped about six inches ... and stayed there! It was over 600 pounds without the money in it. And there was a lot of it in there! Later, we found out, over $950,000 in cash! One guy got in the back, re-covered it with the blue tarp and we loaded up for the trip back to the phone company; ... I mean to the storage unit we had arranged. Ya know ... where it would be a "safe" safe. (I promise, dat'll be da last fuckin time! ... Really!)

OK! ... Looks like we did it! ... A tan Datsun, 260Z, with three guys in it, just went by the driveway and slowed down. I don't like the look that guy had on his face when he looked at us. I got a real bad feeling abooot dat ... ehy? (Sorry; wrong story). I was driving. As I started to pull out of the driveway, I saw the Datsun, turning around, in a hurry, down the dead end street we were on. I said something's wrong you guys; I can feel it. Those guys are cops! We've been made ... for some damn reason. Maybe, it was a suspicious, nosey neighbor that called'um?

Now I've pulled out onto the road. The Datsun pulls up alongside of us. The guy in the front seat points a shotgun at my (adorable) face! He's only six feet away! The guy in the back jump seat; a .45 automatic!

He yells "Pull over dirt bag!"(Obviously watching way too many stupid cop shows on da telly). (dat's British talk for TV). Then he says "Keep your hands where I can see'um!" The moron's in a Datsun 260z sports car; we're in a large pick-up truck about two feet higher than them. I said "I can't do both!" I told my nephew and Excessively Proportioned Raymondo not to make any sudden moves and to hold their hands up, where the clown could see them, so he didn't defile my adorable face with a damn shotgun blast, causing me to "splash" upon them! I hit the brakes, gently and started steering ... with my elbows, hands out the window, fingers spread, till we stopped! Then I said "Dirt bag?!?!? ... There's no need for name calling, ya know". (I was gonna add, you little greasy palmed asshole! But he still had that damn cocked .45 pointed at my face. I thought it best to resist that particular temptation at that particular point in time lest we had an "accidental" weapons discharge). Ronnie, our idiot in the back jumped out and took off, downhill into the deep woods; with a cop in pursuit ... of course. Now, plain clothes cops (and I mean, really fuckin plain. These guys really had no eye for fashion ... <u>at all</u>!!!) were on both sides of the truck. We got out; they frisked us for weapons; me leaning against the truck; arms and legs spread wide; .45 auto at my head! They couldn't do that with Ray, he would've tipped the damn truck over; then separated us (because ya know ... ya gotta keep'um separated).

There's four cops, three with shotguns, one with that damn .45, all pointed at me! They make me stand in the middle of the road (I was always an "independent" anyway, so that, really didn't bother me), then kneel down with my hands behind my head. Someone says "Lay face down and spread your arms and legs wide, like an X". I said "O'key dowkee". Now five cops are standing around me in a wide circle, each about ten feet from me; ... possibly, ten feet nine inches (it's hard to get an accurate measurement when you're lying on your fuckin face). Like they thought I was gonna explode or sumtin. All pointing shotguns at me! If the dumb asses shot me, they'd of hit each other too! ... I had no problem wit dat part. I assumed they'd cuff me quick, but now I'm lying there in the hot sun for a good five minutes, trying not to get my face burnt on the blistering hot, melting tar of the macadam road. It's about 95 to 100 degrees by now; I look to my side an there's my pet 500+ pound Grizzly. They had to "chain" four pairs of cuffs together to cuff his hands behind him. He looks at me; then says to the cops surrounding me "will somebody cuff him and get him off that damn road before he fries?" I said "Ehy, I'm done on this side ... You can always grill me more back at da station!" Then, one of them approached me from the rear (I'm glad he wasn't gay), knelt on my back, and did it. Later, we found out from, Frank T., the head of their task force, they were afraid to come near me because they had been hanging around my school, watching classes from the vestibule (or maybe they were just talking to our friend in Texas ... or my girl ... Lois Lane). They took us, all in separate cars to the Westchester County Jail, in Yonkers. We still didn't get how they knew; or even why they were even there. We were in that damn place, separated, for seven days. The guy who took off for the woods was caught when he tripped and fell (a typical city guy, from Yonkers or "Yunkus"). The cop chasing him stomped on and broke his ankle for running away. His toupee came off (no, not the cops; his stayed on)! We didn't even know he had one!

The whole damn thing was a fuckin mess! When they first brought us into the jail, they called the homeowner; the guy who hired us. Then I knew we were in deep dodo, because we had almost no direct contact with fecal head; no proof. Most of our contact was through Ernie. They brought the safe into the police station. One cop, McDonald (who also owns a chain of very successful cheap, shitty burger joints), talking to another cop, said they needed him to come down, claim and open it! We were all sitting there in cuffs; I said "Lemme tell ya how dis is gonna go. Dat repulsive stool specimen'll come in. He won't even look at us; like he doesn't know us, and refuse to open the safe." McDonald said "Why?" I said "Because I've been trying to tell you guys, <u>it wasn't</u> a real robbery! You got it all wrong! I already told you why we were doing it; <u>for</u> him. But he's not going to hang himself with his wife and the IRS. He's gonna throw us under the bus!" He said "Why won't he open the safe?" I said "He can't let you know what's in it." McDonald instantly said "It's full of drugs!" I said "No, it's full of cash, and now he's gonna make like it was a real robbery ... Did you check his front door?" He said "Why?" I said "Because it has two very special heavy duty dead bolts that can "only" be opened with a key ... from either side. It's a very expensive special door and locks! Was it broke? ... He left it unlocked for us, so we wouldn't have to damage it, to remove the safe. Just watch him when the slime ball comes in. He'll totally ignore us and try to get his safe back." He did ... and ... he did!! McDonald said "Son of a bitch, you were right on the money! I said "No ... it's still in da safe". He wanted his safe, butt (< I had one of these left over from the other story) refused to open it. "OK ... now remove these damn cuffs; cut da shit and drive us home. I got a lotta shit ta do!" He laughed; I liked McDonald, he had a good sense of humor ... for a fuckin cop (but really lousy burgers)!

We were still trying to figure out howda hell they knew about it. Shortly after, we found out from our group lawyer, Bill, through disclosure laws, they had our phones tapped, for many weeks. I didn't discuss anything about this shit on the phone ... with anyone! Yet, they knew exactly, when and where (you remember the yet ... again, from the Canada One story. Please ... don't make me go true dat again; cause I still don't know where da hell it is). Then we got it! Big Ray's phones were tapped because they, the task force, ran it back from the big bookie, in NYC, who they were after for his illegal gambling operations, whenever he called in bets for his bookie business. Then back to my martial arts school, gun shop and home; also, to my idiot nephew, who kept calling the Large Bruin, asking him "When we were gonna doda job." That's how they knew! They just picked it up by accident. The cops pieced a story together ... for themselves, thinking it was a real robbery / hit! That's why they were there waiting in such force. There were thirty of them (twenty nine for me ... and one for all the other guys! At least that's how they made it seem.) They had the entire street blocked off at the end, with multiple, layered police cars, thinking we were stupid enough to try and plow through them, we found out later. Now they even knew about our buddy in Texas, if they didn't already. A simple, effective, precision operation turned to shit because one gabby, moronic asshole couldn't keep his damn mouth shut on the damn phone, like a gabby old lady! I wish ta hell they'd a shot him!

Ronnie, the guy with the broken ankle put up his house as collateral and finally got all of us bailed out, after a week. The cops didn't like that. We were not allowed to leave the state, nor our own county, or have any communications with each other. We did anyway, but not with phones. There were no cell phones back then. (We used smoke singles, <u>in Spanish</u>; from the Cuban cigars Ray smuggled in from Canada ... ehy). A friend I had working in the local post office, told me every piece of my mail was being opened and checked, by authorities. So, I stopped using my POB for anything but bills, and wrote or told everyone not to communicate with me, with mail, even on holidays or phones anymore, until it was cleared up (even my most be-loved, outta state, ex-girlfriend; <u>that</u> really hurt the worst!). I feared the "law"; possibly even the Fed's would start watching them too, since Ray and I had been working inter-state too. I didn't want my problems to involve them in any way, even if they weren't doing anything wrong ...... or even if they were. I'm an outlaw; always have been; I expect trouble; but I can't let the shit that hits me, splatter on my innocent loved ones. They matter too much.

The Large One and I were told to report to the area HQ-IRS office in White Plains to be questioned about the whole damn mess; but mostly about the money in the safe and owner. The safe still wasn't opened. Those guys are really paranoid! They have a private parking lot in the rear of the building with a tall metal fence surrounding it and although they gave us the buildings physical address, neither inside or out, nothing says IRS or US government; anywhere! You can't find it unless you go to the information center inside and ask. We had to tell them who we were and they would call up to confirm we were supposed to be there. When we finally found it on the third floor (an unmarked door), a little, sandy haired Irish guy, came over to question us. The little guy was the "Big Cheese" in that huge office. Not yet knowing exactly what he was, but recognizing him instantly, I said "Hey man, we went to High School together, also in White Plains; just before I got thrown out. I could see that made him visibly nervous. He denied it! I said "Don't worry; take it easy, I understand; but we were in homeroom 2H together. They nicknamed it Little Italy, because it was 95% Italians. It was also the "troublemakers" home room ... go figga. You were in the front corner seat, right by the door; and you took attendance!" He finally conceded (I never forget an Irish kid). Then we talked about the case ... and that rotten Catholic school; and the silver suede shoes I always wore ta class! (They never forget great shoes; especially the Irish kids). We told him the truth; exactly what happened, and he was pretty cool with it. That nauseating turd of an owner, who hired us, then tried to cast us beneath a large, public mass transit vehicle, to cover his own ass, was the one they wanted anyway. Good thing I remembered about that damn $2,500 door; it made all the difference. Our super lawyer, Billy T., used it to convince them what really happened. We still didn't know how much was in there either, but eventually, it was found to contain well over $950,000 cash! They finally opened it with a federal warrant. Not with the actual warrant itself, that's only a piece of paper; they got the combination from ... Oh, fuckit! ... It's none uhya damn business anyway!! ... Go fondle ya *yet*!!! ... (If... ya can find it). *******

... *Great Legs for a D.A.* ...
The "*Vicious*" Interrogation!

OK, nearly one year later, after many court appearances and postponements, we're now entering the grand finally of this stupid side show. The task force had been trying to put enough crap together to bake us alive, even though now they knew the truth of the incident; but, they had to account for all the money it cost. The hundreds of man hours of surveillance and phone taps, over many weeks, it cost the state and counties they were working in. Not to mention the unwarranted, vicious verbal attack and aspersions, cast upon a fine upstanding "Dirt Bag"..... as myself. I for one, will never be the same ... ya know. They got a couple of bookies; some info on a guy in Texas, from my phones, and an IRS cheater. Apparently, we unwittingly, committed a misdemeanor. As it turns out, it's even illegal to "fake" a crime in the worthless, idiot run (Mario Cuomo) overpriced, shit-ass state of New York, whether you report it or not! ...... WTF!

One by one, we were called into the Westchester County, District Attorney's office for a vicious interrogation (no waterboarding though ... they just did the floors). I knew they had already questioned The Large Bruin once, a few days earlier, but that was all I knew (we ran out of Cuban cigars to send smoke singles in Spanish with) except, they weren't done with him yet (Don't Start!). They assigned me a "clown" of a court appointed attorney, with whom I appeared at their main interrogation room. A real joke; he sat away from us, in a chair in the corner, as if he had no idea what was going on; and I could tell, he really didn't! He never even asked me about the charges or case and it was obvious, he couldn't care less. So, as usual, I was standing alone ...Well ... sitting. As I walked into the room, I saw a long table with 6 men and one attractive 35-ish woman with glasses. I smiled, greeted everyone nicely and said "You can't all be here for me! I'm not that important ... to anyone!" Ask my girlfriend. The woman was the Assistant D.A.. She asked me to sit at the head of the table. I told her I'd be honored, but I couldn't believe all these people were here just to see me. The County D.A., Frank T. the Westchester County task force leader, who arrested us, and the head of the Dutchess County drug task force were there as well as her. I don't know who the others were … and I really didn't give a flyin shit (<See, good things will happen, if your patient)! I believe some of them were from NYC, investigating the murder of that poor kid in the airport parking lot I mentioned in chapter one (remember, they thought I was a hit man) and likely more of them. I'm not sure why they did it. Maybe as a distraction or maybe they always did it, but the attractive assistant D.A. sat facing, right next to me, on my right; acting very stern. It shouldn't be this way, but I know women have to act tougher in a world controlled by men. Inside, I could tell she was really a sweetheart, but she had to act tough for "da job"! Besides, she had a short dress and great legs; an I'm a "Leg Man;" have been since I was … 5. Even with their pants on, I could tell … the men didn't! They probably didn't shave them either! Anyway, she started asking me questions, but what surprised me was, so far, there were absolutely none, about the phony burglary. She started asking me about names I'd never heard before; in the city, I assumed. Then she played a phone tapped, conversation between Big Ray and me. I, as usual, was injecting a bit of profuckinfanity in the phone conversations; so I looked into her pretty eyes and apologized for it. She said "It's OK, I'm used to hearing things like that." I said "It's not OK with me. I still apologize; you wouldn't hear it from me. I might have a nasty mouth, but I don't normally use that kind of language around women." She said "Thank you" and nodded her pretty head, with just a tiny smile. Now, it was just her and me; no one else mattered. She asked aboot (sorry … those damn Canadians infected me for life) the kid in the car at the airport. I told her it was horrible, but all I knew was what I heard on the news (I wish she'd stop rubbing her pantyhose together and pointing her hot legs at me; she's makin me crazy … an hungry)! She played portions of conversations with Ray about the Texas deal, where I said I still wanted ta "Do the guy", when he got out of prison, for what he did to that young girl; if that was OK with her father. They took it to mean "Kill

him". I said no, and told her and them I wasn't a hit man, but I wanted to break both his elbows for hitting her, and crack his nuts for raping that young girl, so he could never do either again; to any woman. I saw another slight smile come on her face, when I did. I realized why two hours later, when 5 of us, moved from that conference room, into her office. I saw a picture of her with her two adorable little daughters on the wall by her desk; it hit home for her. Me too! I told her how beautiful they were; they must take after their Mommy. I wasn't playing her, they really were; I love little kids; especially little girls. And their Mommy was being very kind to me, even in those circumstances. The questioning began again as soon as we all got in there. They knew about the large amount of cash the Texan offered me. He did repeat the offer on the phone to me, several times. They picked it up on the taps when he called me. Even they figured out he wanted a hit man. I've gotten up to a grand a day in cash, many times, for dangerous body guard work, but not the kind of deals he was offering. That's why they asked me questions about a number of hits in NYC. My clown of a lawyer was sitting right next to me now. Frank T., head of the task force, asked why I didn't take da job, for that kind of money. It probably wasn't prudent, but I said "I got no problem killing other men for the right reasons; but I won't kill anyone for greed or money, no matter how much it is. I can be "a killer" and I can be "cold blooded", if necessary, but, I'm not a cold blooded killer! I hope you can understand what I'm trying to say. But if you can't, I don't know how else to explain it. I'm not dat smart". Now, for the first fuckin time, since we got there, my court appointed "super lawyer" speaks up! He's got a very pensive look on his face; gazing at the ceiling and says "Sooo ..... you wouldn't kill someone for a million dollars, even if ...... no one knew?!?!" I froze; they froze; all looking at him with small smirks on their faces. He had a look of total bewilderment on his face, as if he couldn't even imagine someone doing that. I turned slightly toward him, then back at them, shook my head and said "Yeah, and I'm on trial?" I repeated what I said;

then explained there's a "big" difference between killing "for money" and getting paid to fight or kill for a good reason. That's what soldiers and good mercenaries do; even honest law enforcement personnel. The other is cold blooded murder! I turned to Frank and said "Frank, you carry a gun and you get paid. Do you go around killing every chance you get because you're getting paid? If you have to kill, it's for a good reason .... not the money! When I put it to them that way, they seemed to understand my values. I said I answer to a higher authority then men or their stupid laws. The D.A. said "That's very profound Tony." I said "Yeah; Profanity was my major in high school." It took a second for them to get it, but they all laughed, especially her. As far as I know, they never knew I used to be a mercenary. She however, pulled out a folder with my military records and complimented me on my fine service and my "Airman of the Year" award, for risking my ass for others, with total disregard for my own safety ..... as she put it; while I was a sergeant in the Air Force ... (ours). It seemed a silly thing to me that had nothing to do with anything that was going on ... So I slapped her really hard and told her ta shutdahell up, or I'd turn her over an spank her pretty, bare ass if she bought it up again! .... (OK, I didn't; I just wanted ta see if you wus payin attention?) This one's more boring than the others. No killin, no sex, hardly any profanity ... why dahell am I even boderin? ... I'm havin a hard time stayin awake, while I'm typing dis wit my trigga finga! .... I gotta go get some fuckin coffee ....

.... OK, I'm back ... dat's a little better... Nothing perks me up like a hot cup-a granulated liquid caffeine solution, wit bovine mammary secretions and granulated cane powder; (well... perverted sex) ... Now, I can be wide awake ... and bored too! Now, after I blew off the stupid award thing, as nothing, they started asking questions about my 500+ pound pet bruin, Raymondo. Did I buy him? Meet him in a yoga class?? Or just run into him face first, in a drunken stupor... thinking he was a building?? Apparently, he was not very cooperative with them and talking nasty, telling them to, basically, "go shit in their hats!" I told them "He's not really that mean; it's a smoke screen, he's all heart and a big, gruff teddy bear! (Like ... Baby Bartholomew ... <u>Don't!!!</u>) She smiled and said "I know". I said "Even now, if any of you needed help, he'd be the first one to offer." Again she said "I know." She was a very perceptive woman, with a great ass and hot legs. It was easy to see why they picked her for da job (not just for her hot legs and butt, but I'm damn sure they helped!). They asked if he ever had a real job or was he a carrier criminal. I said "No, he's always had real jobs as long as I've known him. When I first met him he was working in a local pizza place down the street from my school, for a long time." He was only 250 pounds then. Then the D.A. said "Anything else?" I said "Yeah, but I can't really tell you." They said "Why, was it illegal?" I said "No, but I'd really rather not tell you." They asked "Why not?" I said "Because you won't believe me ...... and you'll laugh; then you'll never believe anything else I ever tell you!" They denied that they'd do that; both individually, and as a group. I said "Each one of you, look me in the eye; the same way I do when I talk to you, and promise me, you won't hold it against me (well ... maybe you could hold the assistant D.A. against me) and not believe me anymore; or laugh! They did. I said OK ...... I'll trust you; I hesitated a few seconds and said "I really don't wanna tell you this .... He was ...... a roofer!" The instant they heard it, they all burst into hysterical laughter...... she was tearing; except for my lawyer, who never saw my five hundred pound Buddy. He just sat there bewildered ...... fondling his yet! I said "Ya know, for such big deal law abiding citizens, you guys ain't much on keeping your damn word (I really loved making her laugh because she always tried to be so serious, and she was so damn cute; glasses and all). Now you're gonna think I'm lying about everything. I'm losing what little faith I had in the legal system. Not that I had much." I swore to them it was true, but he had to leave da job because he destroyed all the ladders. He bent all da rungs; even doubled up! They were afraid to let him, actually walk on the roof itself. Every time he stepped on a ladder rung, with two eighty eight pound bundles of shingles on his shoulder, it was almost 700 pounds! So they had to let him go. I said "Now! ... Do ya understand why I was so skeptical about telling you? And you reacted exactly like I said you would."

Then the subject came up of him being a "Drug Dealer", because he sold a little marijuana ...... OK! .... A LOT!! A few dozen lousy bales!!! But they didn't know dat! Hey; who hasn't?!? They were making as if it was a capital offense to use or sell it. Again, I looked them straight in the eyes and said that I didn't even consider a guy who sells pot a drug dealer. Crack, coke, pills, heroin, crystal mec are <u>drugs</u>, that kill kids and adults; that's a filthy, slimy "drug dealer" that has no regard for human life. I wouldn't even have anything to do with someone like that; except maybe ta kill'um! I said "How old are each of you here? And be totally honest; like I'm being with you. Because I know I'm older than anyone here, except maybe you" to the D. A.. They all told me, and as usual, I was right. He was two years older than me; everyone else, even my nincompoop lawyer, was younger. I said the only reason weed wasn't legal, was anyone could grow it anywhere, and our filthy, greedy, slimy, no-good, crooked government couldn't tax it. Amazingly, <u>they all agreed</u>; even Frank T. of the drug task force. I said "It's really an honor to be among such honest people. No matter how this goes, I thank you for that." I really respected these three people for their honesty (and her legs, which bought up ......other things!) and I hope they did me. Then I added "Now, please look me in the eye again and tell me if any one of you hasn't smoked weed when you were younger... or yesterday." Absolutely, no one did, but there were a few smiles. I said "So please, stop talking to me about pot, like I'm a sixteen year old, because that's insulting to me, and you." We assumed my lawyer was stoned already anyway. I told them the worst, most common drug of all was still alcohol. Most of the people I was young with got tired of weed and stopped. Most of the drinkers, turned into chronic alcoholics. Then I said "I'd bet my life, every one of you will have a shot, beer or glass of wine after work today..... or smoke a joint!" Again, no one argued. It seemed to me like I was dominating this "vicious" interrogation. I didn't know why, but it was OK with me. I told them when I was a bouncer, in different bars and clubs; I constantly threw out violent drinkers. But I never once had to throw out a stoned pot head; they were always peaceful and causing no trouble. At that point, they said we were taking a short recess (probably tado a bowl). I said "Oh goody! Recess!! I grabbed my lawyers sleeve an said "Come on, push me on da swings"! She looked at me with the cutest giggle ... they all laughed. I think she hadda go pee-pee. At this time it was just Frank T. and me in the room. Frank started talking to me about my martial arts school. He said he was in the dark hall watching with some of his crew. I liked Frank; he was honest and straight forward He surprised me when he looked me right in the eye, smiled, and thanked me for "not hurting" any of his men. I told him, I wouldn't have anyway, because I had nothing personal against any of them; they were just doing da job I over pay my taxes for them ta do. And that went for him too. I had no animosity toward any of them, or any of the people in this interrogation; especially her! I told him he should be proud of his crew for not using excessive force to do their job, as many cops often do. Especially, considering what they thought was going on. (Although ... I could've done without the vicious name calling like "Dirt bag!?!")

I added "Besides, only a complete moron would've made any sudden moves, with that many guns on him (and I'm an incomplete ... moron). Whatdahell daya think I am, Superman? He laughed and said "You scared them! ... Me too!" I said "I'm not Superman or The Flash. I can't move faster than a speeding bullet ... or six (possibly an arrow?)! So, thank that bunch of "fraidy cats" for me, for not shooting me ... or anyone else."

Then the questioning continued for about another hour or so. At that point I said "Ya know, I looked all of you straight in the eyes and told you the truth about everything you asked me about; which was more than you did to me, about laughing at Ray's job! I explained that whole stupid, mock "burglary" mess to you; in detail; and to the cops that brought us in that day. Especially about the front door, with the special locks (it's probably what saved us; proving the set-up), being left open for us; something they didn't notice until I brought it up and they went back to investigate it. There's nothing more I can do. If ya wanna send me ta prison fa dis crap ... go ahead! (At that point Frank said "Please ... don't call me goat head!) You know as well as I do, I'll go in, be a good boy; then, as soon as the first oversized, tattoo covered, muscle headed nitwit gives me a problem, I'll kill'im; in less than the blink of an eye ... and then ... <u>all</u> his slimy friends! After that ... I'll own the damn place!" Frank looked me in the eye, well ... both of them, gave me a big smile, nodded his head and said "I know". I was kind of sorry when it ended, I was having a lotta fun; amazingly enough, it was extremely interesting. The whole damn thing took a bit over five and a half hours ... (Well ... not counting the torture ... ya know?). God what legs! But I couldn't lick'um! Dat was da real torture.) ***

Me and Big Bear ... *On Trial?* ... Is This a Multiple Choice Your Honor??

Ok, so they finally want me to report for pre-trial, which probably means I'm gonna spend a year or so behind bars. Not drinking or bouncing ... jail bars. I don't know anything about The Big Bear yet (other than he's Big ... and I won't discuss his yet). They're doing me first (I wish the assistant D.A. was). I figure I'm going straight from the court room in cuffs to a cell. So I tell everyone I'm gonna be real late for dinner; "Real Late, So start without me!" The Westchester County Court is huge. There were at least a hundred or more people in there. The judge's desk or whatever the hell they call it is huge! It was about ten feet high, probably because there were so many people and they didn't make us go up in front of it. You just stood up when your name was called. So you always had a clear line of sight with the judge, where ever you were in the courtroom. To my right was a jury box, but it wasn't filled with jurors this time, just spectators and lawyers. On this day people were only there for sentencing or setting their trial dates. I didn't know in advance which I was there for. In that jury box there was a group of people. Among them, in the very first row, by the door, were the D.A. and his attractive Assistant D.A.. I didn't expect them. Anyway there were a lot of cases before mine. I was really getting tired, bored and about to tell the judge to shake his fuckin ass! I had better things tado! But ... I refrained (dat's 6). Then, finally, the judge called my name. I stood up; he asked if that was my name. I confirmed it (I wanted to say "Ya called it didn't ya ... dumbass?! Why da fuckin hell else would I stand up?! Daya see anybody else standing, besides dat stupid cop?! But again ... I refrained (< Holy shit! Dare it is again, dat's 7!) He kept glancing down at the papers in front of him. Then he asked my age. I replied "forty seven, your honor." He looked down at the paper in front of him, adjusted his glasses and looked back up at me, from his "pulpit". I was about twenty three feet ... six and a three quarter inches in front of him. Then he did it again, slowly, never saying a damn word. I turned my head down and to the right. I could see the D.A. and her, already smiling and watching me, a few feet away. I rubbed my chin, pensively; then I turned back to him ... and with a question in my voice said "fortyyyyyy six!????" He looked back at me and nodded his head ... so I asked "Is this a multiple choice your honor?" He said "This is serious Mr. Zerro!" I said "Sorry your honor; I forgot ... I was sick a year." I could see him biting his lip, trying not to break. The courtroom came apart with laughter. She came apart at the seams. (Well, she was wearing nylons). The D.A., laughing himself, had to take her by the arm and help her out of the courtroom her glasses in one hand, the other covering her mouth, tears rolling down her pretty face. Anyway, I only got a "G" fine, an A misdemeanor and a year probation. I'm sure she had a lot to do with that. But it was worth it just to see her laugh that hard! To this day, Big Ray has always insisted she seemed to have "a thing" for me. I didn't think so. He said he realized it when they were questioning him for the second time; after me, the next day. Ray said all her questions were about me. I don't know what that "thing" might have been ... Well ... but if so, I'm damn glad she had it (I wish she would'a gave me dat ting privately).

When it was over, I came out of the court room (didn't seem to be much point staying there. I didn't see any food, TV or sleeping facilities. Besides ... I didn't have my teddy bear... Baby Bartholomew ... __Don't!!!__). They were both standing out there in the hall talking. As soon as she saw me, a big smile came on her face (Nooo! Do that one on your own!! ...You disgust me, you filthy pigs!!!) and in her pretty eyes (I said "__NOOOO!!__"), shaking her head from side to side. I went over to them and thanked them for being so easy on us; even though we really didn't do much of anything. I shook the D.A.'s hand; then she stuck hers out, I took it up to my lips and kissed the back of it (I wanted to lick it but ... I refrained. OMG! Dat's 7!); then gave it two more and said "Give those to your two beautiful little angels, from me, when you tuck them in tonight". I wanted to kiss her too butt again I refrained.

(Dat's 8!) She looked into my eyes, gave me a beautifully warm smile and thanked me. I said "I'll miss you ... not him ... just you"; smiling and gesturing with my head toward the D.A.; he smiled and shook his head too. She really was a sweat heart. I knew it! And ... I really do miss her too.

A couple of days later, I found out The Big Bruin got sentenced to one year, even though he only got charged with an A misdemeanor, same as me. But it seems he had a felony nine years and ten months before. After ten years it wouldn't have made a difference. He only missed it by "That Much". His first day in, some muscle headed idiot started up with him ... saying he ran the fuckin (< I hadda get at least one in) place. Ray sent him to the prison intensive care unit, where he spent the next week. They put Ray in solitary for the rest of his time in ... So he wouldn't kill anyone ... Ya know? *******

*Pileated means "hairy" Goddamnit! Try reading a book without dirty pictures, for a change!!!

*A true fuckin story by: Tony Fuckin Z

The Romanian Connection *or Tanks* for the Memory ... *Tiger!*

In the early 90's I saw a great movie called Kelly's Hero's, starring Clint Eastwood, among others. One of my favorite all time flicks. One night, comedian Don Rickles, who played one of the movies main characters, appeared on the Johnny Carson show, promoting the production. He told about the miserable conditions he and the cast had to endure for 8 months in Bucharest Romania, where most of it was made (gee, I can't wait ta get me some'a dat). As it happens, my new business partner, Constantine, was from Bucharest. Constantine and his family escaped from the brutal Ceausescu regime, with a price on his head (only $39.99; they didn't really want him that bad), before Ceausescu was over thrown and executed, along with his entire family, on the main boulevard in Bucharest, shortly after the Russians left. Constantine was a very gifted designer/artist who designed, built and over saw the production of the giant ornate iron light posts on the main boulevard in Bucharest. It's gigantic, about 2 miles long and about 200+ yards across (the boulevard, not Bucharest; that's much bigger). He and some of his old buddies back home kept in touch for years. I found out later that Constantine, though not a musician, was instrumental in helping plan the execution of the overthrow. Constantine was famous all over Europe for his work. He and they, had great connections in Romania, but with the new dictator, it was still a dangerous place, still mostly closed to the outside free world. All that power made him paranoid that the same would happen to him. Constantine and his buddies were ex-Romanian commandos, who used to work with the Russian military when they occupied Romania. His friends, who I eventually met, got high positions after the overthrow, since they all took part.

My interest's there were multi-fold; I wanted to produce a super survival knife and a knife / belt buckle for a money belt, both of which I designed. But mostly, I wanted to buy "Tanks"! Yeah ... tanks! German

Tigers left there by the Nazi's after WW2, as well as the American Sherman's, and other armor I saw in the movie. Most people can't tell one tank from another. Most war movies are made using modern tanks, with re-painted insignia's for that reason. I knew exactly what I was looking at. They were real! Almost none of the most well-known; most notorious tank that ever existed remained intact. They were the scourge of the European battlefield; and they had at least three; also a lot of Sherman's and half-tracks we left there. That's why, along with the ruins that still remained, they made most of the movie in Romania. Germany only built about 1300 Tigers. Most were destroyed in the African desert. It had the biggest gun, the notorious 88mm and the thickest armor. For a long time they were impervious to almost anything the alias threw at them. A very few are in the collections of multi-millionaire military collectors. I could get at least a cool million or more apiece for them back in the states.

The key here was connections; they had them (I used to be an electrician, but shockingly, my connections were useless here). INOX, the oldest company in the world is now based in a huge building in, what is now, Bucharest, Romania. INOX is over 2,000 years old. It descends from the Roman sword, knife and armor smiths that traveled with their Roman legends; then stayed and "mixed"... if ya know what I'm sayin, with dem Dacia tribal chicks, that they conquered there. That's how Romania got its' name. INOX is also the mother of all the knife companies, in the modern world. INOX is now run by two guys, Sandel and Buduleachi (Note here: They weren't the original owners); two of Constantine's closest old buddies and business partners. They knew people and people who new people! But first we had to get there ... and back. Especially BACK! Romania just came out of Russian communist rule and occupation. Relations with the free world were not the greatest; especially with Mr. Slime Ball himself, Bill, piece-o-shit, Clinton. The new dictator was cautiously suspicious of everyone. There were armored trucks, tanks and troops with AK-47's everywhere. I'd feel a hell of a lot better if I had one too.

The whole damn trip was nuts, starting with the plane ride; right from the airport. Constantine had to go three days ahead to make arrangements with the others and make sure things were in place, for my ten day "vacation" in this winter wonderland. Romania was the real Dracula's home town; King Vlad the Impaler, a real sucker and a Goddamn, Royal pain in the neck. When he arrived, he called me at my karate dojo office (not Vlad ... Constantine) to tell me what to bring. To be more specific, what we needed to bribe our way around and endear myself to his friends (as if my great looks and charm wouldn't be enough). Starting with a Remington 870, 12 gauge pump shotgun, for the head of, what is their CIA. They wouldn't tell me his name. They're not available there (not names; they have lots of those), only AK-47's! Fortunately, I was a licensed FFL dealer at the time. As well as 2 cartons of Marlboro's. Another half dozen cartons of Marlboro's for Stellieko, the head of all Romanian customs. Two more cartons each for Sandel and Buduleachi and a liter of vodka for each of them. Fortunately for me they have a duty free area at the Bucharest terminal. I was surprised they even had a terminal. Damn it! Dis is gettin expensive! They really like Marlboro's there. Maybe the Marlboro man should'a been a Romanian instead of a cowboy; or at least a Romanian cowboy from western Romania! Constantine told me you can't get any sweets or sweet baked goods there, just bread, because there's no sugar. So I got 12, baker's dozen (13), boxes of Dunkin Donuts, (maybe I should'a just got sugar instead) to bring for "the troops". I had 3 G's in hundreds hidden under the sole inserts of each boot and another in my pocket; also my American Express card; I wouldn't leave home without it. It's the only card accepted in Romania (what a fuckin honor). I also brought 10 rolls of toilet paper. A few people told me, it's hard to get in Europe. That was for me! They cut down all the trees over the last millennia. They use old crepe paper, purchased from the USA. It's in most home bathrooms. Tuff sphincters!

Speaking of assholes, however, the real shit started back at Kennedy airport, when I wanted to check my bags at Romanian airlines. Now let's see ... it's an airport, I have a gun, in a box, going to a country ruled by a dictator; I'm alone and I don't speak the language! What a great fuckin combo! What could possibly go wrong??? There's a real chunky, New York City, street talking, moronic nit-wit, African-American woman running the booth, as well as her big damn mouth. So before I attempt to go thru, I quietly try to inform her of what I'm transporting, so as not to cause a stir (or arrest!). She immediately, very loudly, begins running her stupid fucking mouth with, "You gotta gun in dat box?!" As if I'm trying to sneak it thru. She's turning around to all the other workers, alarming the other passengers, rolling her eyes, throwing her hands in the air saying "I need security here!" After 5 minutes of commotion, two cops come; frisk me while I'm trying to explain to them that it's a gift; in pieces; in a taped up box, that's supposed to be carried in the cockpit; instructions that came directly from Romania. And no, I didn't try to sneak it on; and the idiot that has now made almost an hour of commotion about it, should be shot in her fat ugly face with the damn thing! The place was packed, but I finally got the Romanian head stewardess, in a short, tight blue uniform (I'm not gonna do that one, (and her) but I really wanna!) and asked her to please take my gun (nor this one) and bring it up to the pilot. She said she couldn't do that. I gotta say "She was <u>HOT!</u> (That's why I really wanna do the bunns ... sorry, puns ... but I won't; cause I got way too much fuckin class fadat shit!) She was in possession of <u>unbelievably</u> magnificent legs ... and she had <u>two</u> of um! With a perfectly, <u>delicious</u> looking rump!!" With <u>matching</u> cheeks!!! I'm getting hungry just thinking about it (I think she was the real "Devil with the Blue Dress on" Mitch Ryder was singing about!). Everything changed when I finally convinced her it was for the head of their CIA. I really felt so bad because her... so pretty little face looked so terrified and with a tremble in her voice she said, "Wait ... I go talk to pilot!" OK, but I really don't like seeing women scared. Five minutes later she came back; took the box and said, "I take into cockpit." (Nahhh ... I'm really not touching dat one. Dis is killin me I tell ya).

The flight was long; over 9 hours, but the head stewardess was very nice; giving me anything I wanted; well ... almost (I wished she'd live up to her title. I know, I know; I'm disgusting and no damn good; nuttin new)! They wear short tight blue dresses, sheer pantyhose and spiked heels. That will make the flight seam waayyy too short! Like her uniform! Anyway, later I realized she was being nicer to me, than everyone else. They're pretty short with the passengers on that airline (fortunately, that also applies to their clothes). But it seemed like they were used to it, and didn't expect much. I guess that guy waiting for me in Bucharest, scared the shit outta these people (Maybe, I should'a offered her some toilet paper). That raspy, sandpaper sound a woman's legs make when their nylons rub together, always makes me Nuts! And Hungry!! It's like a dinner bell! (In fact it makes my ... no ... I can't ... I won't!) It was as if she knew it, and was trying to turn me on. I knew she really wasn't, but she was leaning over me and her incredibly perfect, nylon covered legs continuously brushed and leaned against the back of my hand (I wanted so much to turn it around). Oh no! Now my tongue's getting stiff! I was in heat now, so my head wasn't working; at all!! I felt like I was wedged against the back of my seat by something pushing against the seat in front of me! ... Well ... at least it "felt" that way. It's a good thing I didn't have to stand up! Not positive; but I believe pole vaulting is illegal on commercial aircraft. The guy sitting in back of me asked for a drink and she said, "NO!" No reason, just "NO!" Later, the guy across the aisle asked for a blanket; it was pretty cool in that cabin (I thought they'd at least have a wood stove); she said, "NO!" But a few minutes later she brought me one ... with a pillow; I didn't even ask! When she left, I gave it to him. She made some of the guys around me put their carryon luggage (why people put their good stuff in dead animal carcass I'll never understand. For God sake, buy a damn suitcase! They're not that expensive! The stink was unbearable!) on the floor between their legs to accommodate the multiple duffels with boxes of donuts, I'd piled on top of me. She carefully, loaded them into the overhead compartments. I don't think any of them even considered complaining about it, watching her do it in what little there was of that uniform. Sure as hell not me! (It was more like a long T-shirt). If anyone did, we'd have all piled on and beat him to death anyway! Her dress rode right up above the bottom of her ... perfect bottom. The last hour of the flight was real pileated (No! Not again. Go look it up, dumbass!). It was early December; real cold. The wings were icing up pretty badly. She was the only thing that took our minds off it. The heat she was causing probably melted some of the ice and saved our lives. The landing was real rough, the plane was twisting and sliding side to side, but when we finally stopped I witnessed something I never saw before in all my years of flying, including 8 years in the Air Force ... (ours). The entire plane load of passengers exploded into applause for about a minute straight; whistles and all! Maybe, they don't make it down in one piece that often? Or maybe... it was for <u>her</u> (I'll choose door number two, Bob). Romanians are nuts. No surprise to me after working with Constantine for the past year. Now I forgot why I came. I don't want to leave her; ... I can't!!! I just hope Romania has only one plane; so I get the same one and crew going home ... I really miss her.

Constantine said he'd be waiting at the terminal when I arrived. Damn it! I don't see him. Romania is the only place left in the world where they still speak almost pure old Latin. I don't!! Everywhere I look there are troops in camo with AK's. Normally I don't mind that; if I have one too. At least I could get a couple of them before they dropped me. Even the airport personnel are all military uniformed with side arms, including the two guys looking down at my papers, up at me and back down, again and again, with rotten suspicious looks on their faces; mumbling to each other in their shielded booth. There're a few hundred people here; I've been holding everything up for over 20 minutes. Well, the two suspicious soldiers checking my papers were. But I didn't hear any passengers complaining. That's not a smart idea in a place like this. Where the hell's that obnoxious, fat, little bastard? Did he get arrested? I haven't heard from him in 2 days. Did they kill him? I don't speak Latin! Ya know I got Trouble ... ah say I got Trouble, right here in BuchaCity ... with a capital T and that rimes with Pee and Goddamn it! ... I really gotta!!!

Then I heard a familiar little voice yelling from the waiting crowd, "Tawny! Tawny"! Normally that voice irritated the hell outta me but this time it was music to my ears (Nooo ... not like Music Man). It was Constantine! Amazingly, nobody killed him ... yet. I gave him hell for being late but he said as usual, he got drunk on vodka, with his old friends the night before; and the one before that ... and the one before that, when he first got there. When he reached me he had some of his friends in back of him, including Sandel. When they stepped out of the crowd the two soldiers in the booth shot up to attention as if they had rockets stuck in their asses. They stood frozen, staring straight ahead. There stood Stellieko, head of all Romanian customs. He stood about 5'8", with a cold, menacing, Gestapo officer look on his face. Could it possibly be that ankle length black leather coat he was wearing? Or the matching black leather cap with the badge in the center? Nahhh ... I just thought I was in an old WW2 movie. He never said a word; just waved his hand, as if he were back handing someone's face. The two soldiers quickly closed my passport and papers; then handed them back to me without a word; then went back to attention. A few yards away, out of our immediate sight, two other troops had already opened all my baggage, on a long, large metal table, along with the doughnut bags. The inspectors reacted the same way, when they saw Stellieko. Again he waved his hand and they quickly closed everything up. I gave him one of my carry bags with two boxes of doughnuts and two rolls of toilet paper. I really don't know which he liked more. He'll probably use the toilet paper one sheet at a time (both sides). I shook his hand (before he used it), then went to the duty free area to get all the vodka and Marlboros; came back; gave Stellieko his. Then I finally saw a smile break on his stone cold face. He was eatin a fuckin doughnut! I almost choked to keep from breaking into hysterical laughter. He had white powdered sugar all over his face, like a little kid ... Sooome Nazi!

Meanwhile, someone else had arrived ... with his assistant ... again in, a full length black leather coat ... of course. Maybe it was standard issue for scary WW2 type guys. He was the head of, what is their CIA. All the others seemed real glad to see him. Like ... they were "gettin da band back together"! The guy the head stewardess and pilot seemed so afraid to piss off (I really miss her). He seemed very nice, but again, no one would tell me his name. He smiled, shook my hand, then talked to his old friends in Latin for a few minutes (All that Latin; I was having flashbacks of being an altar boy again; except for the child molesting priests, of course). I gave him two doughnut boxes, vodka, Marlboros and a Remington shotgun. I thought he was gonna have a damn orgasm; or... maybe even tell me his name. But den he would'a hadda shoot me wit da shotgun I just gave'um!! He heartily thanked me with a big smile, shaking my hand, with both of his, so damn hard, he almost dislocated my damn shoulder. Then I turned around to talk to Constantine for a moment. When I turned back ... he was gone. Disappeared! Like ... Keyser ... Keyser Soze!!!

Sandel drove us back to his home in a car the size of a soup can (condensed). All those boxes and luggage were piled in the back seat with / on me, thru absolutely the worst traffic jam I've ever seen. Down that insane main boulevard, packed solid with a couple million tiny little kitty cars, eight lanes across; on each side! To a giant traffic circle in front of the humongous capital building (one toilet, in the basement); we were in the center lane, half way around the circle. I still had to urinate; really bad and I'm claustrophobic in crowds. The jam was incredible; we couldn't even open the doors. I could've reached thru the open window and slapped the guy in the car next to us, if I wanted to; and I did, but he probably would'a got mad. They hate when Americans do that; ... Belgians too! Those fuckin people are NUTS!!! Yeah! Even the head stewardess! But I wish I was stuck in there with her, instead of them ... I really miss her. We were stopped dead there for over forty five minutes, before the traffic even started moving again. Sandel said he and Buduleachi set up a meeting with two guys that might possibly get us the Tanks, two days from now at INOX. Meanwhile, they took me to meet Romania's ex-ambassador to the U.S. A real rich asshole; by their standards! Actually, he was an asshole by any standards; only rich by theirs (I think he used toilet paper for a napkin). He spent a lot of time telling me how much he disliked the USA. He complained about the heavy bombing of the oil fields at Ploesti during WW2; the main source of fuel oil for the German war machine. I told him, you just picked the wrong side. If you're gonna make an enemy of someone, make it someone important; and why wait? You might as well get right to it! We needed to deal for some materials for the knife production and he wanted the business. He also had complaints about American processed foods ... in a country that had <u>no refrigeration</u>. We spent most of that day with him, listening to him bash the USA. I was getting real fuckin tired of it. He kept talking about how the food in Romania was always "fresh". I reminded him about the lack of refrigeration. You couldn't find a vegetable anywhere and the meat stunk because it was starting to rot! At one point we were walking on the sidewalk in Bucharest; again he was running his fat, stupid face about the U.S. when I cut him short. A stray dog (I'm just assuming he was; I didn't ask him if he had a home) was dropping a large, wet, brown pile on the sidewalk a few feet in front of us. I said "Look! Go ahead! Get your face in there! Take a big bite!! ... It's fresh!!!" That was the end of the conversation and our business attempt with him. Go figga? Sandel got the D3 tool steel we wanted directly from Germany ..."They" have refrigeration.

Bucharest was one of the craziest, dirtiest and ugliest cities I've ever been in (OK, OK ... it's not Newark, N.J.; but it's almost as disgusting). I don't know how the people get around in it. None of the streets are marked. All the buildings look exactly the same; plain multi story gray concrete, same size, same shape. All the windows are the same type and size. Everything is covered in dirty black soot. You can taste it in the air and it makes everyone cough ... a lot! It's caused by the only heat these people have; portable kerosene heaters in their homes or apartments. Only the wealthy have any type of central heat. In the morning, thousands of people fill the streets carrying large cans to get them refilled at distribution centers. At night it's tough to sleep because the streets are filled with huge packs of barking stray dogs; fifty, sixty or more in packs. They were let go by the residents, who could no longer care for them; then multiplied (or divided), after the mess that occurred when the Russians left. In the day time the individuals are everywhere. Then they pack up at night like coyotes. Outdoors, the need to side step dog shit was constant. I saw an empty lot, about an acre or more, completely filled with a pile of garbage, about fifteen feet high, because sanitation pickup had ceased; huge rats running all over it. They're probably what the dogs were feeding on. The stench was incredible and it was December; the dead of winter! No place for a summer vacation! They had NO refrigeration ... anywhere. Even in the "fanciest" restaurants, one of which they took me to. I pitied the poor residents, but it was in some ways like a bad comedy (ya know ... like this one). They took me to, what they said, was the "Best" place in town, for diner. There were no more than a dozen (not a baker's dozen either) people in there including us. What I took to be the owner; came and took our order. There were only three choices on the menu. None of them had any vegetables; again, no refrigeration to keep anything fresh (maybe they should've had dog shit on the menu;

no shortage of that). The top choice on the menu; special of the day was Salisbury steak; a big hamburger. OK ... I can dodat! I ate plenty of grubs, snakes, monkeys, scorpions, parrots, etc. in the jungle, while I was a mercenary). The place was dimly lit. I think that was for the better. Nobody in their right minds drinks the water, if you can even find any! Then the owner / waiter presented us with what seemed to be his pride and joy. He pulled a gold cord with tassels, to draw back a maroon velvet curtain and reveal a large metal ... Coca Cola sign! There were a bunch of bottles of this "American Champagne" on the table, in front of the sign. I could see he was popping the buttons on his chest, with pride about it, so I complimented (Constantine translated) his restaurant and him as well. However, it's not so much the Coke-a-Cola, but a product they make, that these people were so damn crazy about. "Fanta", which looks and tastes like ... sweetened piss!!! Please ... Don't ask me how I know what that tastes like. Everywhere I went after that; even at business meetings; "hot" secretaries (amazingly, in mini-skirts and leather boots, like it was a secretary uniform) would bring out trays of champagne glasses filled with it. Then, with pride, the head honcho would always say, "Fanta". Of course I would smile and reply, "Oh, wonderful", while in the back of my head thinking, I love drinks that taste the same going in, as they do coming out.

The Salisbury steak was ... OK. I ate it all. Probably the best thing I had the whole damn trip. There was one slight catch, however, I had to go wee-wee again. OK, where's the pee-pee parlor? Ah, right over there! As I approached the door, I noticed a bit of an odor coming from the porcelain facility room. It got much worse when I entered. There were six separated stalls with no doors. One of the workers was just coming out as I was entering. As I looked into each of the stalls, I discovered the source of the odor. Each had a mountain of, need I say it, piled up about ten inches or so, higher than the seat; which I'm sure no one sat on in quite a while (I hope!); probably since the revolution. NO toilet paper! Hey, ya know ... I can hold it! There was NO running water in the sinks either. Hmmm, that was probably the cook! ... OOOhhh God! Was that really ... Salisbury steak?!?... Check please!!! ... No! Hey, I'm good! No dessert for me thanks, I'm tryin'a cut down on dat shit; literally! Besides, It might be ... chocolate pudding! Get me da fuck outta here! The damn jungle was cleaner than this place! I'll eat when I get back to the states ... if I make it. I drank a lotta vodka that night ... Disinfectant! ... An I hate vodka!!!

I heard a lot of automatic fire right down the street last night. AK's; real close-by. Don't know what it was about, but it lasted a good ten minutes ... Somebody didn't go home.

Finally, the meeting at INOX! Tanks be ta God. We got to INOX about nine in the morning. Mangy dogs and dog shit everywhere. Sandel brings us in, all the way to the top floor (about 6 stories), no elevators; tiny steps, like they were made for elves. The meeting was in a back room, of a back room, of a back room; down a long dark hallway to another back room! It was like a maze. I'd be amazed if I could've found my way back out. I should'a bought a compass! (We passed some human skeletons on the way in. I think they didn't make it.) Sandel locked each of the doors behind us. (I hope there's no fire. I didn't see any smoke detectors coming in).These guys are so damn careful. But in this shithole country, I really don't blame them; or mind! There was a T76 Russian heavy tank right out front, just across the street, when we came in. Buduleachi was waiting in the last room with two guys. It was the first time I met him ... and them. Holy shit!!! That's the biggest human I've ever seen ... in person! Buduleachi then introduced me to the two underground Russian arms dealers. One was about five foot four or so (I've changed baby diapers on kids bigger than him); the other was easily seven feet tall, about three hundred fifty+ pounds! He had at least another ten pounds of gold chains around his neck, not to mention a couple of enormous gold and diamond rings on both hands (too late, I already mentioned it). A freak that's freaky about freaky jewelry, among other things. How freaky? They looked like Mutt and Jeff. When they stood together, it looked as if a giant cannibal brought his lunch! The skinny little guy couldn't have been a hundred ten pounds ... maybe? What a sight they were. From here on, I'll refer to them as the big guy ... and his lunch. Then the big guy immediately started talking to me in Russian. I pointed to my ear, smiled and shook my head no. Everyone in the room spoke multiple languages, but my Italian, English and Japanese just wouldn't cut it here. I understand a lot of Latin and Spanish, because it's the Italian origin, but these guys talked so damn fast. We sat at a rectangular table and began conversing to decide what common language we'd deal in. They decided on French; I hate French! But they all spoke it. Many years ago, when I was a trained mercenary, out of necessity, I could understand and speak some ... badly, to a point. French is still the most prolific language (not to mention most nauseating ... Opps! Too late again!) in the world because of French colonialism. Many Native American tribes even spoke it. We had a little edge here with these two shady characters because they would have little conversations about things we said or asked about, in Russian. My people made out that none of them understood Russian.

They spoke to each other in Latin, which the dealers also understood. Then Constantine explained to me in English. Well ... his version of English. It was all very confusing. What the dealers didn't know was he was also fluent in Russian, understanding all their private little conversations (He spoke 6 languages; just not all at once). It gave us a nice edge. First, of course, I asked about the German tanks. They didn't seem to understand what the hell I was talking about. Buduleachi got them there thru his connections, asking about tanks. They told him they could get them; but he failed to tell them I was looking for the German Tigers I saw in the movie, made just outside Bucharest. They were there to sell me brand new Russian heavy tanks right from the factory in Russia. It was the time the Russian government as well as their economy was in utter turmoil (and yet ...

there wasn't a confused cow in sight!) and pretty much collapsing so things disappeared all over the place. The Russian underground was having a field day (hot dogs, beer, soft ball, tanks an all). I asked if the tanks were like the old T76 across the street. They said no, they would be a much newer upgraded model. It was food for thought (I just hope not from that "shitty" restaurant) because I knew I could find buyers for them, but I knew they would have to be "de-gunned" if I tried to get them into the USA for collectors. But I wanted the Tigers. One thing made me real nervous. These guys kept telling us they could get us "anything" military that we wanted; like truckloads of AK-47s, RPGs; even nuclear materials! That meant that anyone else who had the money could too. The world was in a lot of turmoil at that time, especially in the Middle East. The offer was more than interesting, but scary! So I asked for the only thing I wanted more than the Tigers. I told Constantine to ask them if they could get me the airline head stewardess ... I really miss her. They smiled and promised they'd work on it ... I knew they understood.

The meeting lasted over two hours. About an hour in Sandel went to a small closet and pulled out some refreshments ... OOOhhh! Whoppy Fuckin Shits! ... Fanta! (Just what I needed, more Coca-pee-pee!) The big guy's lunch said they'd try to locate the three Tigers and if they were available for sale. I knew they'd tack on a healthy finder's fee for themselves if they did but I also knew it'd be worth it. At this point I made an important phone call while there, to a friend back in the states. He said for sure, he'd have "out of the country" buyers; friends of his, in South America, for the Russian tanks. We could get at least a half million plus for each of them. They were only asking fifty thousand USD each; delivered, on flatbed rail cars from Russia, right to the docks! At least the trip wouldn't be a total loss. However, I stipulated they'd have to throw in the head stewardess, or no deal. Some things are worth more than money ... I really miss her.

The entire meeting Constantine was translating for me in English. OK, we're done for now. Buduleachi brings out a bottle of Russian vodka to celebrate, and hopefully, wash down that ... Goddamn Fanta! And I Hate Vodka! We all toasted ... a couple'a times to close the meeting. We got up; everyone started shaking hands; the big guy's lunch shook mine, smiled and said something in Russian (nooo ... not the actual word "something"; Something else; I don't know what da hell it was; I said I don't speak Russian, damn it). Now the giant cannibal did the same. He shook my hand, with a big-ass smile; then clear as day said, "It was very nice to meet you Tony, and I hope we can do more business together in the future"... Son-of-a-bitch!!! Then we all finished off that bottle of vodka ... <u>then another</u>! Then we all laughed our asses off about it. Of course, later we all re-attached our asses for future use! Ya know ... In case we ever wanted ta make complete assholes of ourselves ... Again!

No Tigers, but a successful and interesting trip none the less. I got my buckles and knives. I got to meet and bribe a lot of high ranking government people in another dangerous country, see Transylvania, Vlad the Impaler's (Dracula) castle, the wall with the bullet holes where the entire Ceausescu family was executed, a lot of wild dogs and dog shit; I insulted an international ambassador, ate in a restaurant with no running water and an open septic tank for a bathroom, saw a lot of beautiful T34 Russian tanks, deal with devious, rouge Russian arms dealers, drank a lotta Fanta-piss an vodka and got back alive. Tanks be ta God ... But I never did get my incredible ... head stewardess. NO! I'm still not gonna do it. Besides, I'm sure you already did your own ... Wow! Dat's even more disgusting; and it would just be too redundant; over and over and over again. And you'd hurt your back! Butt Damnit! ... I really miss her. *******

Constantine, like most of my old friends, is gone now. I'm sure and hoping, I'll see him again, soon. His legs weren't nearly as great as hers; sure as hell not his ass, but I miss my little Buddy too. I told him a hundred times to stop smoking those Goddamn cigarettes before they killed him! But he didn't; and they did. He had a thick head, but I loved that little shit. He taught me a lot (mainly to stay away from crazy Romanians), we did a lotta "stuff" together; we had a lotta fights and a lotta laughs ... I really miss him too. *******

*Another true fuckin story by: Tony Fuckin Z *

Read more "True" short stories; with the adventures of Tony Fuckin Z, (until he dies of writer's cramp ... to his right index finger!)

About the Author

Author, Tony Zeno, is a high ranking Martial Arts Instructor (Sensei), ex U.S. military, and survival guide.

Mr. Zeno has lived in numerous U. S. states for 80 years.